UNDERSTANDING AND COPING WITH GRIEF- 2 BOOKS IN 1

HOW TO MANAGE YOUR LIFE AFTER THE LOSS OF A LOVED ONE

CORTEZ RANIERI

CONTENTS

10 HABITS FOR GRIEF AND LOSS

LIVING WITH LOSS

10 HABITS FOR GRIEF AND LOSS

CREATE CHANGE THROUGH ADVERSITY TO BECOME A BETTER YOU

DEDICATION

For my late mother, Maureen Ranieri. Not a day goes by where I don't think about you. I'll cherish the time we spent together for the rest of my life. I love and miss you always. I'll see you on the other side angel.

INTRODUCTION

It was November 24th, 2007. I was abruptly woken up by my aunt. Her eyes were filled with tears as she struggled to get the words out, "Cortez, she's gone. Your mom has finally let go, and she's passed away." I rubbed my eyes, continuously opening and closing them, hoping I was in a bad dream. It turns out, I wasn't. Reality had set in and my mom's two-year battle with cancer had finally ended. This was a day I knew was coming but could never fully prepare for.

As I walked upstairs into her room, my family surrounded my mom's lifeless body. They all looked back at me with tears in their eyes. My knees became weak and my chest tightened up. As I got closer, I saw my mom lying on a hospital bed with her eyes closed. I kneeled beside her, grabbed her hand, praying she would hold mine back, but there was nothing. This reassured me she was gone. My eyes filled with tears as I laid my head on her chest and said my last goodbye. I was 14-years old at the time and I thought I was prepared for this, but fate proved me wrong. However, I saw I was not the only one in grief. Despite feeling lost and struggling to breathe through my overwhelmed chest, I resolved to do everything I could to heal and, perhaps, help those around me heal too. Since then, I've lost all my grandparents as well as two friends and have learned many things about death that I want to share with others.

Grief has a remarkable tendency to make us feel alone, yet we're never truly alone in knowing the experience of grief. Death is one of the most frequent causes of long-term grief, but it is not the only one. Maybe the love of your life abandoned you. Maybe your parents split up, and now live a world apart from each other. Or maybe you've recently begun living thousands of miles away from a childhood friend you used to visit every day.

It does not matter if the cause of your grief is big or small compared to those around you, you're still allowed to feel the associated guilt if you think you could've done something better. You're still allowed to acknowledge the sense of helplessness if the cause of grief was never something you chose. You're still allowed to experience regret if you did choose, only to wish you could still go back. Most of all, you're allowed to feel alone, even if you spend each and every day in a room full of people. Loneliness isn't determined by how many or how few people are in a room with us. It's determined by who we wish was still there.

However, all these feelings are only one side of a coin. You wouldn't be reading this book if you weren't willing to try and get back to how you used to be before your tragedy happened. You won't ever be like you were before; instead, you'll be better. Helping you achieve mental clarity and helping you nurture your inner strength is my primary concern throughout this book. I resolve to help you regain control over your life. Imagine a life where you are strong despite your wounds. Imagine a life where, even though you may feel helpless from time to time, you're able to recover and make the best of what's left going forward. Imagine a life where your pain ceases to be nothing but a reminder of what you lost; imagine a life where your pain can become a way for you to reach out and comfort those you love. But first, imagine a life where you are able to reach out and comfort yourself.

To these ends, I will show you ten strategies, each of which are geared towards strengthening your soul. You will learn exactly how to take the pain and adversity in your life and transform it from a debilitating problem into an opportunity for growth.

If anyone has ever frustrated you with the words "misery builds character," only to then leave you miserable on your own, I will show you how to persevere until those words transform into something more helpful. Suffering alone does not promote growth, but what you'll learn shall ensure that your pains will not be for naught.

But why does showing you all of this matter so much to me? Why is it so important that I share all I know about dealing with grief? As I said, I felt lost and overwhelmed after losing my mother. I tried a lot of things; I tried talking to people, I tried not talking to people. For a while, I barely ate at all. I indulged in stacks of comfort food, like heavy, high-GI (glycemic index) carbs and sweets. I've tried music, and I've tried silence. In the beginning, I was just a kid. It took me many years to come up with a system that worked in soothing my grief.

After testing many, many more habits as I was growing up, the ones I've finally included in this book are those that I continue practicing, even as a fully-matured adult. Even after coming to terms with my grief, what's written in the chapters of this book continue to help me in my day to day life. Because of this, I strongly believe that these ten tips will help you, too.

The reason I share them with you now is that I know not everyone has been able to take the time to figure things out in the years since age fourteen. Let my trials help you heal, and hopefully cut a clearer path through a confusion similar to the one I once had to walk through.

Now more than ever, it is important that you make time for yourself, be gentle with yourself, and most of all, show care to yourself. For some people, grief is an illness that must be eradicated. For other people, it's simply part of the human condition that needs to be understood. Regardless of how you view grief, it's important that you take some time to maintain yourself. Join me now, and we'll start somewhere simple; maintaining your body.

1

MOVE YOUR BODY

One of the easiest ways to maintain your body is through exercise. To some people, exercise means working yourself to death, performing several laps around the block, or climbing to the top of a tall rope. This is not what we're aiming for. We are exercising not only to get more fit but to clear our heads.

Now, exercise will not snuff out your grief, but it is still essential for helping you cope with loss. Physical exercise is one of the best ways to release endogenous endorphins into your bloodstream. When released, these endorphins help your body cope with pain as well as help your mind find calmness. Unlike alternative methods of numbing pain, such as alcohol, your endorphins are not addictive, will not impair your awareness, will not create delusions, and will never cause feelings of dependency. In reality, because your endorphins are a product of your body rather than an external crutch, using their natural release to boost yourself is one of the most empowering things you can do in times of helplessness.

It is no wonder, then, that exercise is often suggested as a healthy way to combat depression. However, it's not as simple as that. For a start, grief and depression are not the same thing, even if society at large tends to use the two words interchangeably. Medically, depression is indicated by persistent sadness and a noticeable decrease in pleasure from life or activities, including hobbies you normally enjoy.

Depression can mean slower movements, indecisiveness, apathy toward death, loss of hunger, poor sleep, or an overwhelming feeling of worthlessness, paranoia or guilt. You do not need to be conscious of what's making you depressed to experience depression and, the more severe your depression is, the more of these symptoms you'll experience at the same time (Knott, 2017).

Grief, meanwhile, is explicitly an intense pain caused by the feeling of loss, especially when it's the loss of a friend or loved one.

However, grief can turn into what's medically termed as *complicated grief*. *Complicated grief* is defined as a powerful physical and emotional reaction to a loss that persists for a long time, potentially even years (Smith, 2018). Symptoms are largely similar to those of depression, with the added bite of experiencing intense pain whenever you think of what you lost. Complicating the matter is the fact that, during grief, it can be difficult to think of anything else. It's no surprise that experiencing such intense pain for so long can easily cause a downward spiral into depression itself.

Exercise, then, lets you deal with grief while preventing you from being swallowed up in complicated grief and, by extension, depression. However, even if you are already exhibiting symptoms of depression, do not fret. It's not too late to start getting your endorphins going and erode the malaise of despair.

Even as little as one hour of exercise per week can help alleviate the effects of complicated grief or depression (Harvey *et al*, 2017), allowing you to tackle your true grief in an uncluttered, healthy fashion.

HOW TO BEGIN: THE MINDSET

Of course, grief is deeply taxing not just on a mental level, but on a physical level too. The intense sadness we feel in response to loss can leave us feeling exhausted, on top of shutting down our normal self-care routines. When this happens, how on earth do we galvanize ourselves? Where do we find the motivation to begin exercising again? What if we never exercised even before the grief?

The trick is to start small. An hour is only 60 minutes. That can be broken up into 10-minute bouts across 6 days of the week, with a 1-day sabbath. That's half the length of a kid's cartoon show per day. You could even spend those 10 minutes of exercise in front of the TV while watching a cartoon show, if that's what you enjoy.

Grief does not affect us all in the same way, so choose something that's just a slight tad outside of your comfort zone. If your grief has caused you to shut yourself in isolation, allow your exercise to be a brief walk to your mailbox and back. When you return to your couch, your bed, or wherever you sit when you contemplate your grief, consider performing a stretch before laying down. When you engage in exercise, you help take your focus off your pain for a little while.

Now, when you're grieving, it is understandable that you might not want to take your mind off your loss and, by extension, you might not want to do anything that shifts your focus. You might even see shifting focus as bad. Consider why you might feel that way. For me, I found it difficult to shift my focus off my grief because, on a deep level, I felt that if I took my mind off who I lost, then I'd lose them completely. Of course, this isn't true; even after all these years, I can remember the way my mother's laugh made me feel, or the memories I shared with some of my late friends as we speculated on our futures and dreams. But, at the time, I was adamant that I wouldn't do anything that resembled actually letting go.

However, sometimes a shift in focus is exactly what we need. Shifting focus is what lets us take a step back and get a better view of the big picture. When we experience *complicated grief*, we trigger two things: the "reward" parts of our brain, and the "avoidance" parts of our brain (Jewell, 2014). In hindsight, this explains much of why I felt as I did at the time. I was constantly longing for the "reward" of seeing my mother again, every time I thought of her. But, of course, that reward would never truly be satisfied. I'd see pictures or videos of her, of course, but those never felt fully like *her*. If anything, they just highlighted her absence. But still, the "reward" part of my brain kept flashing, creating a yearning.

Eventually, I became addicted to the thought of her presence. Now, I wasn't ready to confront her loss yet by any means, blame the "avoidance" part of my brain firing up all the time, but working out helped me get closer to where I needed to be.

For a while, I exercised entirely on my own. The "avoidance" part of my brain kept me away from other people. I couldn't bear the thought of perhaps one day losing them too. At that age, it didn't occur to me that by cutting myself off from everyone the way I had, I'd effectively lost them all already.

The shifting focus caused by my exercise sessions slowly helped me realize how self-defeating my thinking was. Before this realization, I'd sometimes spend about a quarter of an hour walking around a field near where I lived, ruminating on how awful life was and how worthless I felt for not being a better son. What I didn't realize at the time was that the more I kept walking, the more I was telling myself that I still had some power over my body. No matter what was on my mind, I could still trust my feet.

I considered the world I was walking around in. I didn't really want to be in it. I never asked to be in a world without my mother. That wasn't my choice. But it was my choice to walk around in this field. It was my choice as to where I'd put my feet next. More and more, I began to visit this field, until I was there almost every day.

More and more, I gradually began to feel at least on a subconscious level that although I didn't like where I was, or where I'd been, I could still decide where to go from there. For a while, I began to feel a little better. And then winter came.

During winter months, when the rain was too intense for walks, I let myself go again. I thought it was just the winter making me feel worse, but it was the lack of exercise. However, as walking felt too cold, I started to run instead. I ran to the nearby library and did sets of stairs. Although it was freezing out, my body quickly warmed up from the intense exercise. When I would return home, my *monkey mind* would be completely settled. I spotted the connection between my physical activity and sense of peace.

When I eventually figured it out, I joined a local gym. I wasn't particularly knowledgeable in working out, but after enough time shifting my focus off my grief I began realizing my body ached like hell, and not from the exercise. The strain my grief had put on my body left me feeling like an old man, and I was only in high school! I hated stretching, it was too boring for me, so the best way for me to scrape all the rust off my bones, was to create a routine. I began doing a little bit of stretching every morning when I got up, and sometimes just before I had a shower too. It didn't make me feel happier, or less anxious, but it did make me feel *better* in the sense that things didn't feel so impossible, and at that stage that's all that really mattered to me: believing that life could still be possible.

Maybe you're not a fan of lifting weights or running, but even so, I'd highly recommend at least giving yoga a try. Now, it's not something I did when my grief was at its worst, mostly because I still hated stretching back then, but when I passed into adulthood and began taking a proper look at what it meant to do yoga, I began cursing myself for ignoring it in the past. To this day, I like to perform a mini-yoga session in my bedroom before getting dressed in the morning.

TOO MUCH OF A GOOD THING

Although galvanizing yourself to perform exercise can be helpful, you must be careful not to overdo it. While a little exercise will help lift your mood and regain perspective, you must remember that your body is still hurting while you are in grief. You do not want to exercise to the point that your pain becomes worse. If you had a strenuous workout routine before your loss, do not shame yourself for letting it go. Taking a step back and giving your body a little space to rest is probably the smartest thing you can do in this case (Frey, 2019).

If you're used to rigorous physical activity, then you are more than welcome to continue as long as your body isn't fighting you. For some people, staying true to their routine is even a way of finding solace and maintaining a feeling of familiarity or security in a world that may otherwise seem very precarious. However, you are not under any obligation to continue that routine.

No matter how stringent you normally are concerning your exercise, one must note that while you are grieving, you are naturally more vulnerable to illness, clumsiness, injury, tiredness, muscle pains, and back pains. Even highly well-trained individuals such as veteran infantrymen are known to suffer from these physical symptoms while they are working through grief. If you are not performing to the same standards that you used to, do not fret. This isn't a sign that you're losing yourself, or that you've washed up. Reduced performance is natural in a time like this.

When you have not yet come to terms with your grief, it's comparable in many ways to suffering from an illness. Would you try to push your body beyond its limits while you're suffering from an illness? Failing to meet your usual exercise targets during this time does not mean that you yourself are a failure; all it means is that you're still recovering, and that's okay. Just keep doing the exercises you can. You want to feel the air fill your lungs. You want to feel a warmth spread through your muscles. You want to feel your head rarify. But you do not want to feel pain.

If you're a hardcore fitness enthusiast, you may be used to the idea of treating your fitness obstacles like brick walls for you to bulldoze through. However, right now, you are not a machine. With all the water in your body, you're an ocean. Perhaps, right now, you're a sea of tears. Take a moment to consider the ocean. It can gather up with mighty winds to become a devastating and powerful hurricane. Yet how long does that hurricane last? After a few days or less it dissipates, and the land undoes its accomplishments easily. In the end, all the hurricane does is inflict injury before fading away.

Now, consider the ocean when it is calm. It moves back and forth, rising and falling, in a gentle rhythm across the world. Yet it is this gentle rhythm that carves pillars out of the earth, builds land, defines mountains and valleys. Therefore, when you choose to exercise in grief, be like the waves, and not the hurricane. This means you should exercise every day if you can, but don't do it to drench yourself in sweat. Don't do it to burn hundreds of calories of fat. Do it to carve clarity out of your chaos.

BEING LIKE THE WAVES

Whether you're a sedentary individual just getting into exercise, or an iron titan needing to cut back for a little while, you can release your endorphins using surprisingly simple, even gentle, exercises. I prefer to keep things light while I grieve, because it lets me stay fit and get the bodily chemicals I need without straining my body or hurting it further. A light exercise has even led to a better night's sleep on multiple occasions, which was a welcome blessing for me considering how tired I felt all the time while I was still processing things.

For something easy, let's start with a brisk walk. Bring some head-phones and listen to some music or a podcast. Listening to music is a popular pastime, and it's not uncommon for us to turn to it when we're feeling grief. You can put on something upbeat that motivates you to walk or pick up the pace. Having an inspirational podcast can also make the walk more enjoyable, while you're retaining informa-tion and learning something new.

If walking isn't enough, then perhaps you'll enjoy some bodyweight movements or a run. You don't need equipment for this, but if you want to do a short burst workout, make sure you're warmed up first. About 2 minutes of jumping-jacks will get your muscles warm and loose. Then, give yourself about a minute to catch your breath. If you're either motivated or don't feel warm yet, feel free to repeat this process another 1-2 times.

After that, find a clear spot away from any main walking areas, and start doing some burpees. You can add in other movements, such as air squats, lunges, sit-ups or pushups. You could do 10-15 reps of each and repeat this process 4 times. If you want a more intense workout, you can repeat this process or add more reps in 1 session before the energy expended stops being worth the endorphins you're getting back. Make sure to allow yourself a full minute of total rest for every 2 minutes you spend exercising.

Do not be afraid to start small, even if you're known for being a fitness champion before your loss. There is no need to rush; simply make sure you're getting your endorphins each day. Even if you're doing much less than what is suggested, don't be ashamed. Some days all you can do is a 10-minute walk, or a short stretch before bed. Anything is better than nothing; simply do your best to keep doing "anything" consistently. If you feel safe enough to reach out to friends or acquaintances, see if you can involve them in your exercise routine as well. Their presence will be a great help in keeping you motivated to carry on, although the emphasis is on the word *help*. If you have to go it alone for a while, I believe you can do it.

If you're interested in using weights or expanding your exercise repertoire, do not be afraid to go online to search for things like weightlifting, yoga, or Pilates techniques. If you're able to get out there, join in a local group fitness class with like-minded people and feed off their energy to keep you motivated.

2

EAT WELL

E arlier, I mentioned off-hand that exercise is a better way to take the edge off emotional pain compared to, say, alcohol. But does that mean you shouldn't drink at all? And if not, what are the alternatives?

Diet is just as important as exercise. Similarly to exercise, it is also one of those things that we tend to either ignore entirely or indulge in way too much when we are grieving. If you've lost interest in food as a result of complicated grief, then you've likely lost quite a bit of weight since your loss. On the other hand, maybe you decided to dive as deep as you could into your comfort foods, and have since put on a lot of weight as a result. Some people are more fortunate than others and don't get visibly heavier from all they eat. Others are not so lucky; it's okay to be a little overweight, but social stigmas around the condition can make an already difficult situation even harder from body-shaming.

However, my advice from earlier has not changed; this is not the time to judge yourself. When we are grieving, we already feel down. Why kick ourselves while we're down by adding to the negative voices around us? Weight loss or weight gain isn't a priority right now, regardless of what people around you may be saying. The priority is helping you retain a clear mind. Luckily, exercise isn't the only thing that can contribute to this; a good diet can help you puzzle your way through your thoughts, too.

ALCOHOL, CAFFEINE, AND WATER

The first thing I cannot recommend enough is to cut down on caffeine and alcohol. When we're grieving, we dehydrate ourselves very quickly through the immense volume of tears we shed, or the cold sweats we experience from deep anxiety. Although alcohol is known as a nice distraction, and caffeine is known to give us plentiful energy, both of these substances only give their gifts for a very short amount of time. In the long-term, they can disempower you by making you feel dependent on their effects to have fun or feel alive (Frey, 2019).

What's worse, both of these substances make you pass more water from your body than they give, causing you to dehydrate even faster. This is an issue because over 75% of your brain is made up of water. Think of this water as a cooling system in a computer. If you're dehydrated, then your mind begins to become slower, begins to have greater trouble processing information and, if left untreated long enough, may even begin to overheat or crash.

Caffeine and alcohol, therefore, are not good for keeping your mind clear during grief. But that doesn't mean you can't indulge in any of these substances at all!

Much like the sweets or chocolates that one might have had as a child, unhealthy foods are fine if taken in moderation. For coffee, I highly recommend no more than 8-10 ounces each day before the mid-morning. For alcohol, it is best to have no more than 5 ounces, or 2/3rds of a cup, per week. As an adult, I like to have all 5 ounces in one day on my Sabbath, and then take pleasure from exercise instead during the other 6 days of the week.

Aside from that, I recommend drinking plenty of water. 10 cups a day is recommended. The best way for me is to have a cup as soon as I wake up to help clear my head; we still dehydrate while we're asleep, so it's important to take that edge off with a nice glass of water as soon as possible. I'll then have another cup at breakfast, lunch and dinner, and a final cup just before I brush my teeth and use the toilet in preparation for bed. I'll also have a cup just after finishing my exercise for the day. That's already 6 out of the 10 cups needed. I don't make as big a fuss about counting the other 4 these days, but I do make a point of getting up and going for a drink of water immediately if I'm battling to think, or feeling very hot or dry.

If you're struggling to cut down on the coffee or alcohol, you may wish to drink more water as a way to compensate. Staying hydrated is terribly important for your brain, and without proper hydration you'll have a difficult time processing your grief. Investing in a reusable water bottle and keeping it close by can trigger you to remember to drink water throughout the day.

PROTEINS AND MINERALS

Proteins are a vital part of your diet, allowing your cells to regenerate optimally by aiding in the DNA replication process. When we're grieving, we already feel as if we're under a lot of stress. When we're short on protein, that feeling can be magnified as cells will be more likely to replicate imperfectly or respond poorly to everyday wear-and-tear, causing a vague feeling of unwellness without there being any clear cause (Lehman, 2020). During grief, it can be a good idea to make sure at least a tenth to a third of what you're eating each day consists of protein. This could mean having a little bit of protein in each meal, or it could mean having a lump sum of protein at the end of the day. The choice is yours.

Luckily, you also have a great deal of choice in terms of what form that protein can take. Fish, poultry, and red meats are all wonderful sources of protein that are easily recognizable. For vegetarians, legumes such as peanuts, lentils and beans are a great alternative source. Eggs, yogurt, milk and cheese will also all work well for maintaining sufficient protein levels. When about 20-33% of your diet consists of these foods, your cells will have a much easier time building themselves up, which will help you feel better.

They'll also help you get the most out of your exercise by reducing the negative aspects like muscle strain, leading to a great positive knock-on effect for your physical and mental wellbeing.

Aside from protein, you can further help your body withstand the physical side of grief through taking in vitamins and minerals. This doesn't mean you need medication, of course! Vitamins can be found naturally in many of the foods around us. Spinach and bananas, for instance, contain B-complex vitamins. These vitamins are great at helping you convert your body's energy stores into usable power when needed, and helping you shake off lethargy. Most of the sources of protein listed above also contain forms of vitamin B.

Meanwhile, chili peppers, broccoli, lemons, strawberries, oranges, kale, parsley and thyme are all rich in vitamin C, a vital mineral for bolstering your immune system. Remember, your immune system has a harder time doing its job due to the way your mental stress affects your body while you grieve. Now, you cannot control when you start or stop grieving per se, but you can control what you eat during that time. It can be difficult to properly resolve grief when we keep falling ill, so in this instance, vitamin C can be a great help in letting you endure reaching into the bottom of your heart.

Vitamin D is great for reducing the aching feeling in your bones and can be gained from egg yolks, cheese, milk and salmon. Your body is also able to produce vitamin D on its own when you're out in the sun, which may be another reason why winter might cause your grief to become magnified. Being stuck indoors wasn't great for me during my grief.

Aside from vitamins and proteins, another good thing to look out for are antioxidants, which can be found in most fruits that have bright or deep colors. Antioxidants help your body in a variety of ways, such as reducing the physical stress on your heart, promoting healthy sugar conversion, and fortifying your mental health. They're also great at snatching up loose particles in your body, such as the carcinogenic compounds from smoke or the cell-damaging particles of toxins. If you've been overeating or smoking a lot during your grief, switching up your diet to include more antioxidants can help you regain control over your health.

Aside from fruit such as blueberries, strawberries, cherries, plums and apples, you can also find antioxidants in a variety of beans such as red beans, black beans, kidney beans and pinto beans. Unlike antioxidant-based medication, antioxidant-rich food has a variety of positive side-effects due to the additional nutrients they carry, on top of also being super delicious. Compare and contrast to the side-effects of some medications, which can include heightened depression, lethargy, or muddied thinking. During grief, those are the last feelings we'd want to reinforce, so as much as possible try to get your vitamins through your food instead of your pharmaceutical supplements. If you feel unsure, do not hesitate to consult a doctor to set your mind at ease. In the case of prescriptions, which are not the same as basic supplements and need to be followed to the letter to achieve safe and effective results, do not change or alter the instructions without the aid and approval of your doctor.

PREPARING FOOD AND LOOKING AFTER YOUR DIET

Even when we know what's best for ourselves, it isn't always easy to act on that information. Depending on the stage and circumstance of grief, it may be difficult to stay motivated with a diet, especially if it is different from the food we enjoyed as a kid. Macaroni and cheese, pizza, potato chips and ice cream are all infamous comfort foods. These foods are fine in moderation, but during grief we tend to overdo it a bit. Much like coffee or alcohol, excessive high-carb diets can end up just making us feel worse in the long run, especially high-GI carbs like processed cereals, white bread, corn starch or white rice.

High-GI carbohydrates and high-sucrose treats, which together make up almost all of our common "comfort" foods, tend to feel heavy in our belly, which is partially where that feeling of comfort comes from. Our bodies like to feel full, and the fullness of a good carb can be intensely satisfying, but our stomachs can't always tell the difference between good fullness and bad fullness.

If we fill up entirely on comfort food, our blood sugar levels begin to spike and crash dramatically. Why does this matter? When our blood sugar crashes, we become lethargic and begin to feel listless, or even begin to show symptoms of depression. Our body does not react well when our blood sugar behaves like a roller-coaster, and anything that affects our body will inevitably have a knock-on effect on our minds.

High-GI carbs also have the nasty side-effect of increasing our cortisol production. While cortisol can be good for the body in small amounts, in large doses it can massively increase your risk of complicated grief or depression. The best ways to get rid of excess cortisol are through exercise and socialization. If your stage of grief doesn't permit you to perform consistent exercise or communication, however, then you will need to be extra careful with what you put in your body for the sake of your stress and anxiety levels.

Nevertheless, carbs are delicious, and you might still want to keep them as part of your diet regardless. Brown rice, rye bread, pitas, tortillas and whole-grain loaves are all great alternatives to high-GI carbs, giving that starchy feeling of comfort while having less intense sugar crashes. Combine them with the suggested sources of proteins and minerals for true healthy comfort.

As a general rule, it is best to prepare all your meals in advance. Our grief isn't always at the same level of intensity, but it often feels as if it ebbs and flows without our consent. If your grief is peaking close to mealtime, it could lead to an eating disorder. This could mean desperately getting hold of food based on nostalgia and convenience rather than nutrients. Or perhaps it could mean not feeling hungry at all even when you know you *should* be eating.

By preparing healthy meals in advance, you give yourself the freedom to make food when you're in the best mental space possible to do so. This could mean making tomorrow's breakfast and lunch at the same time you make dinner. It could mean making something during lunchtime, but only eating it later when you actually feel hungry. Or it could mean pre-cooking vast batches of rice, beans and vegetables so that whenever you're hungry you can take spoonful's of each ingredient out and just plop it on your plate, perhaps with a little seasoning.

It can mean picking a day where you feel relatively okay and simply make all your meals for the week in bulk until you're done. It can even mean putting on some soothing music and only making your food while it's playing. If it works, it works. It can take 6-12 months after a great loss to get back into a consistently healthy eating schedule, so do not give up if you're still struggling to get things done through your grief. Simply take the steps you can, and trust that the more you get into healthier habits again, the easier it'll be to stay there.

When you have a moment, make meals for yourself for the future. That way, when your grief spikes up again, you won't be forced to turn to convenience foods or takeout's. By taking care of your future self in this way, you'll have an easier time maintaining a healthy food intake, because those healthy meals will already be ready-made for you. From there, you can comfort yourself through food without having to suffer from a blood-sugar crash.

Another way to look after your diet is by keeping your changes small. Some of us may be able to switch diets to something healthier instantly, but many of us just go with what we already know. This is because, in the first stages of grief, we're sometimes required to make a lot of very difficult choices in a very small space of time. This can lead to us feeling worn out decision-wise, and contribute to that feeling of mental fog. When in this mental state, we don't like to change. Starting small helps you start making the choices you want without having to also fight yourself.

Like with your exercise, start somewhere that is just slightly outside your current comfort zone. If all you can manage is eating ham and cheese on a tortilla instead of on a white-bread sandwich, then simply do that, and let yourself heal a bit more before incorporating more like spinach or kidney beans. Or, if you're a big eater, make the biggest and most satisfying tortilla you can. While still bearing in mind what we've said earlier, get creative with what you put in it. Salmon, pinto beans and cheese with a sprinkling of lemon juice and parsley? Sure, why not?

Another way you can make things easier on yourself while still maintaining some progress is by reducing the daily dish count. For example, use one cup throughout the day for all your drinking water. If the dishes are too daunting and you need the energy for something else, consider ordering a stack of disposable paper plates and eat your meals off those. While this does mean generating extra waste, paper is still a renewable resource. If using paper plates means you'll have more energy to make healthy meals, and be more likely to do other gentle and caring things for yourself, then that extra waste is completely justified. No one we've ever lost would have wanted us to be so miserable after they're gone. Sometimes the best thing you can possibly do to honor their memory is to keep trying to take care of yourself.

CALLING FOR AID

When my Mom passed, I was lucky enough to still have my dad cooking some meals for me most nights. Just the act of eating was often hard enough, and having him around to make the meal for me made it easier to muster up the energy to take a few bites and keep my body going. Of course, the grief was getting to him too, and on some nights, that would mean I'd be cooking for myself. If you live in a friendly neighborhood, you might turn to your fellow neighbor from across the street and work out a temporary arrangement where they produce healthy, ready-made meals for you.

Even if you don't feel like socializing to that degree, you can still gain help by signing up with a meal service such as AmazonFresh, Uber-Eats, Purple Carrot, or Blue Apron. The delivery services would be more expensive than shopping and preparing food yourself, but knowing you can call on these companies on days where things just aren't going your way can help you keep your anxiety in check. Letting others help you in some areas of life such as this can be just what you need to let you direct your energy to other important areas, such as self-motivation.

3

WRITE YOUR FEELINGS DOWN

One of my favorite books from childhood was *Life of Pi*. It's about a young boy who survives a shipwreck, loses his family (his mother, father and brother), and then has to survive being lost at sea on a lifeboat... that he is sharing with a collection of escaped animals from his late father's zoo. One of these animals is a tiger.

This is one of the most extreme situations I can ever imagine a person being in, and most of us won't come anywhere near a level of loss and danger as deep as this. The story is, of course, fictional. However, in this book was an entry from a naval survival guide which read that the most important tool for survival is the mind and, when we're lost or alone with no hope in sight, journaling is one of the best tools for keeping our minds sharp, self-aware, and most importantly, functional.

This immediately struck me as a ring of truth. Ship captains in days of yore would keep a journal, not only to help them keep track of their crew and the general state of their ship, but also to maintain their sanity and self-confidence throughout a smelly, wet, stressful and multi-month voyage. Traveling the world was no picnic when they were stuck with sails and oars.

In the modern age, navigating through grief is no easier. Like a ship in the middle of the sea, we're in a scary and unpredictable voyage with no end in sight. However, just like that sea captain, and just like Pi, you can use journaling as a way to help yourself cope. The benefits are not to be underestimated; if it was possible to distill all the long-term benefits of journaling into a pill or tablet, it'd be regarded as one of the biggest medical advances of our age.

THE BENEFITS

The first and most obvious benefit is improved stress-management. Grief is often accompanied by a sense of helplessness, which can cause great anxiety and despair. The overabundance of stress generated by these feelings greatly increases the risk of complicated grief. However, that is not the end of it. Stress, as we know it, is what happens when our subconscious brain sends out the "fight-or-flight" signal throughout our body. This signal dates back to ancient times, and was evolved to help us protect ourselves when under physical attack. Many of us do not need to worry about physical attacks to the same degree our ancestors did, but our brain still sends out the same signal whenever we encounter something that we consider stressful. This is unhealthy in the modern age because our bodies undergo rigorous changes while that signal is active; our stomach shuts down, our muscles tense up, our breathing rate quickens, and our heart pumps faster. While these are useful changes to have when stressed by a sabertooth tiger, in the modern age it simply means that when we get stressed by work, relationships or grief, our bodies are automatically placing a huge amount of unneeded strain on us to try combat a threat that doesn't exist on the physical level. This can lead to headaches, muscle aches, sleep loss, greater risk of illness, and other symptoms we tend to associate with grief. Stress plays a huge role in how we deal with grief.

However, when we write our experiences down, we force ourselves to put what's happening into coherent sentences. By explaining your own problems to yourself, you build neural pathways in your brain which tell your subconscious that what you're going through can't be resolved through a physical response, but there may be another solution. This results in your subconscious becoming less trigger-happy with its fight-or-flight signal, and reduces the physical wear-and-tear you'd otherwise be experiencing during your grief.

Spending as little as 15-20 minutes journaling each day can be enough to lower your blood pressure and even help your liver function more efficiently (Baikie & Wilhelm, 2005). You might even find your appetite improving after 4 months or less once you begin journaling, as stress may be the reason why you're struggling to eat the way you normally would.

From a psychological point of view, writing sometimes causes us to express perspectives that we'd never considered before during our thinking. This can help avoid misunderstandings, increase self-awareness, find unexpected solutions to problems, and generally let us become more in touch with ourselves.

The reduced stress, overall, is a great help in preventing further deterioration. The reduced strain on our bodies also makes it easier to heal not only physically, but also psychologically. It's easier for your cells to regenerate when your nervous system isn't overworking your muscles, and it's easier to recover psychologically and deal with grief on your own terms when your brain functions aren't constantly being disrupted by feelings of panic, rage or fear.

In the long term, this can lead to faster recovery from further tragedies such as job loss or grave illness. Of course, journaling alone won't cause miracle recoveries, but its usefulness in puzzling out issues and reducing stress cannot be understated. Over time, keeping a journal will prove instrumental in expanding your memory and understanding. If you've ever wanted to sharpen your mind, but haven't found the motivation to learn lately, journaling is also a great tool for that. Remember your days in class. The students who did best in school tended to be the ones who wrote about what they learned in their own words. They kept journals on each subject devoted to interpreting and engaging with the academic material.

When you keep a journal, you're effectively spending time interpreting and engaging with the most compelling subject of all: your own life. No one's marking you or pressurizing you to learn more about yourself and your true place in the world (which isn't necessarily the place people say you should be in), so this journal is simply about getting as much value as you can out of your past and present experiences, so that you may grow and become better at engaging with or discussing what you truly care about.

WHY JOURNALING MIGHT BE ESPECIALLY IMPORTANT FOR YOU

When we're grieving, we often feel the need to tell our story and share it with others. At the same time, however, we may also feel completely alone. Maybe we don't feel like anyone's really listening to us. Maybe they don't have the time, or maybe they just don't have the answers at all. But why should you rely on other people to determine how *you* are feeling? Who better to take care of your broken heart than you?

It can be extremely difficult to explain our losses to another person, even when they are willing to listen, but journaling allows us to explain everything however we want, in whatever order we want. The journal becomes a conversation with yourself and, through this conversation, you help yourself release the burden associated with one's worst memories.

And, because this conversation is effectively always with the same person rather than a group of different people, you'll be more likely to pick up on recurring patterns, leading to potentially life-changing epiphanies. If you have no life-long friend or have trouble talking even to those who know you best, a journal then becomes the perfect instrument in your therapy and self-discovery. Sometimes if you want a job done correctly you need to do it yourself, and your emotional healing is likely the place where that adage is most applicable.

Journaling is also a necessity for picking up the pieces of a scattered mind. Having a history or a self-identity is empowering. When a tragedy happens, it can be easy to forget exactly who we are. After all, our relationships are part of what defines us. So, who are we when a relationship ends? Journaling helps you to rebuild your identity as an individual, as you're now given the opportunity to redefine yourself in a new context. Who am I after this loss? How will I choose to carry on later down the line? These can be difficult questions, but being able to answer them reaffirms who you are after a tragedy, and allows you to remove the more selfish parts of your grief from your emotional trauma.

Through this, you can become more mindful of life around you. Being self-aware regarding your desires can make it easier for you to live in the present while still maintaining a view on the bigger picture. Through this, you can become more confident. When we spend time writing about what we want or exploring why we feel the way we do, we gain greater insights into ourselves that allow us to make better decisions more easily. This is what leads to greater confidence.

Understanding why we feel as we do by spending time writing about it also allows us to process our thoughts and feelings more thoroughly. If you are a sensitive soul, or if your emotions are naturally intense, then diarizing your experiences of grief can definitely help you. When putting pen to paper about your heart, you add a touch of serenity to your turmoil. The brain finds it easier to regulate feelings about anything that it deeply understands. When we deeply understand a person, it becomes easy to regulate feelings of love or hate so that they don't encourage us to behave destructively.

When we deeply understand our own feelings, they feel less intense, even though they're no less present than they were before. This lessened intensity isn't due to numbness or a shutting out, it's simply due to perspective. A two-story house looks big, until you've seen a skyscraper. A village feels crowded, until you've lived in a city. An abusive relationship feels like love, until you encounter compassion. But instead of making our current grief look smaller by placing it beside a bigger one, you simply make your current grief more manageable by placing it beside all the other events of your life, including those times when you were conscious of the pain of others.

TIPS FOR JOURNALING THROUGH GRIEF

The best thing you can do is make sure your journal is convenient, like a small notebook that you can keep in your pocket. If something truly profound strikes you in the middle of the day, you cannot assume that you'll still remember what it was by the time you get to your journal if you keep it at home. By keeping your diary small, you can take it anywhere and note down anything you want as it strikes you.

Next, journaling is best done by hand rather than at a computer, as neural pathways form more effectively in your mind when writing on pen and paper. Save your keyboard and screen for work projects. It doesn't matter if no one can read your handwriting, the only person your journal needs to benefit is you. The next thing you should do is write as quickly as you can. We have a tendency to try to refine or censor ourselves, neither of which is useful when we need to tackle the difficult personal questions of life. Writing quickly helps you put all your feelings down before self-censorship has a chance to even show up.

When you're journaling, you're telling the story that no one else has the time or inclination to hear, and you're telling it to yourself because you know it'll add value to your life in ways that no one else can comprehend.

So, when you write something down, keep your hands going along. When journaling for yourself, do not stop to read back any of your previous lines until you have put down your pen for the day. Do not cross out anything you've written, even if it's because of a spelling mistake. Never cross something out just because you think it sounds odd or because you no longer agree with it. Even if you didn't mean to write it at all, keep it.

Those words are part of you, and crossing them out blocks you from exploring your relationship with them until the underlying issue behind them crops up again. If you write so quickly that you're not even staying on the lines or in the margins anymore, just keep going. The sentences just have to be coherent; that isn't always the same thing as being neat, orderly or grammatically correct. Do not make time to second-guess yourself until after you've written everything down for that day. Simply pour out what is in your heart. When you're writing, journaling is all about getting that maelstrom of thoughts in your noggin down onto some paper.

It isn't about gaining control just yet; it's about being raw and real with yourself. When we deal with our thoughts mentally, we can easily get turned around and go in circles. When dealing with them on the lines of a page, it is much easier to break the cycle and move forward.

Note that your writing doesn't have to be limited to any particular genre. If you want, you're perfectly able to write in song or poetry. Freeform is naturally better, but if having vague guidelines for your syllable counts will help you, then by all means use them. Just remember that syllable counts are comparable to spelling or grammar for the purposes of journaling: a means to an end that should be ditched the moment it gets in the way of self-exploration.

The best things to write about are emotional and provocative memories, but you do not necessarily need to repaint a vivid picture of what went down. A psychological study found that recounting traumatic events, or causes of grief, in expressive or abstract ways brought significantly more calmnessr than trying to recount everything in perfect detail. In fact, those who tried to capture every little detail tended to become more upset, as they'd bog themselves down with a lot of mental clutter that doesn't actually relate to their grief beyond existing at the same time the loss happened.

Write the way that Jackson Pollock, Edvard Munch, or Ernst Kirchner would paint. Don't obsess over minutiae; capture what resonates most strongly with you.

If you wish to take your journaling to the next level, however, write about your experiences in the third person (Stang, 2020). Instead of saying "I" or "me" all the time, try "him" or "her", or "he" or "she". When we write about ourselves in the third person, it becomes easier to see ourselves as a character in a narrative or story. When reading about a character, we like to think about what they're going to do next if they're in a challenging situation, or what they could do better in the future if they recently made a mistake. Getting into that frame of mind where you see yourself in that way can be highly useful. You might even be able to compare your story to ones that have come before; for instance, the classic "Hero's Journey," a storytelling format where a relatable but otherwise ordinary individual is propelled into overcoming adversity and accomplishing extraordinary things after a moment of great loss, tragedy or grief.

The "Hero's Journey," ultimately, eventually peaks after many trials and tribulations with the death or loss of something or someone deeply important to the hero. Luke Skywalker, for instance, lost his aunt and uncle, lost his friend Ben Kenobi, and ultimately lost Han Solo. When he learned that Darth Vader was his father, he also felt that he'd lost the dad he never knew, since suddenly a figure he assumed to have always been good was now vividly dark and terrible in his mind. Learning Vader's true identity and losing Han on the same day was Luke's deepest moment of loss, but that loss wasn't the end.

The "Hero's Journey" continues by allowing the hero to change, adapt, and to try and rectify any previous mistakes. In Luke's case, he rescued Han, he helped resist the regime that hurt his family, he honored Ben's memory by finishing his training, and ultimately, he helped Vader return to being the hero he was meant to be.

The "Hero's Journey" is used to tell stories that are larger than life, but the idea of growth or even redemption after a great tragedy is something nearly universal in the human psyche.

What you endure may make your life feel as if it is burning down around you, but even ash can fertilize the soil for further growth. My mother died, and I could not change that. But I could still grow by honoring her memory. The more I wrote to myself about the pain I was going through, the more I began to understand that this was far from the end. The more I realized I was responsible for my emotions to my mother's death, the more journaling I prioritized.

My writings helped me hold onto all my memories of her as I gradually let go of my grief. Thanks to this, I've been able to get closer to peace and come closer to honoring who she was, rather than mourning what is no longer there. Her body and mind are gone, but after everything I've written about her, I feel as if her spirit is always with me. I've since found greater comfort in my words amidst bittersweet thoughts.

4

MEDITATE

There are many ways to meditate but, when meditating in grief, there are certain rites to be aware of. Before we begin, I want you to imagine a rain cloud. Dark, thick and heavy, it blots out the sun. And there it sits, day after day. A rain cloud does not dissipate until it lets its raindrops loose. Likewise, grief cannot subside if we do not allow ourselves to feel it. While the previous three exercises are all about simplifying grief, this should not be confused with trying to avoid grief or ignore it. Everything so far has been written to help you clear away distractions and clutter so that you can focus on your grief while remaining functional enough to survive. You are a survivor... or at least, you will be.

It is good to honor a person in peace when you're ready to do so. Until then, allowing yourself to experience your pain without self-judging is a way for you to honor your grief. You have a right to cry.

As tempting as it may be to keep soldiering on, you do not need to take on the hard heart of a soldier to survive.

To confront your grief through meditation, take a seat. The best place to sit is on a cushion on the floor, cross-legged. The next-best place to sit is on your bed, cross-legged, but only if sitting on your bed doesn't make you feel unusually drowsy. When you're sitting in this way, remove any coverings you have on your face. This includes spectacles and contact lenses. If it's easier for you to meditate in the morning before putting your coverings on, that's fine too.

Wherever you sit, make sure the room is dry and has light pouring into it. Dampness and darkness tend to wear a person down over time, which causes unexplained feelings of depression. Sunlight is the best light, as it promotes vitamin-D, but any bright light will do if you live in a place that sees little sun.

When you are ready, breathe in slowly. Breathe deeply, so that you can feel the air even at the very bottom of your lungs refresh and detoxify. After you have taken a few deep breaths, let your body fall into a natural rhythm of inhalation and exhalation. Do not try to control this rhythm, but maintain your awareness of your breath. Maintain awareness of the feeling in your chest as your lungs fill up with cool, fresh air, and exhale all that is stale. As you're breathing, place your hand on the center-left of your chest, where you can feel your heartbeat. Keep your hand there, but very gently. Imagine your heart is an infant that you need to cradle; touch it reassuringly, keep it safe, but don't become too firm. Do not constrict it. Don't shut it away. Maintain awareness of your breath, and feel your heart as it expands and contracts in your chest.

Next, when you are ready, begin to recall the memories leading up to your event of grief. If you are not ready but wish to continue in some way, you can do so simply by recalling the emotion instead of the events around it.

Keep your hand on your heart, and do not forget about your breath. If you've been journaling, then this may be a little easier. If you're struggling, don't stress. Grief can already be a struggle, so don't let anxiety distract you from it. If your memories are wanting to come forth vividly, let them. Do not shut them out. Let the narrative, the imagery, and the emotions all build up naturally. Do not force anything. Let it come as it does.

Keep breathing, and keep your hand against your heart. Observe what happens as each emotion comes forward. How does your breath feel? How does your heart feel? How does your body react as you experience love? What about anger? Or regret? If your anxiety hasn't left you, do not fret; simply pay attention to what it is doing to your heart and your breath.

Feel your heart gently through each of these emotions, no matter what order they come in or how long they last. Do not rush; give yourself enough time to deal with each feeling as it arrives. Be kind with yourself. You are part of this world, and this grief is now part of the world's grief. If you need to cry, let your tears fall to the ground. If you are outside, let the soil keep your grief. If you are indoors, let your tears hit the carpet, or the floor. From there, let them evaporate into the Earth's air so that it can keep your grief that way instead.

When you are finished, your grief will still be with you, but you may notice that rather than being a dark and all-consuming void, it is now more like an ebony soil. It is fertile, with a potential for growth and life. You do not have to plant anything in there yet, but through allowing yourself to meditate in this way, your grief will not simply be your opponent; it'll become your partner in resolving an even deeper question.

IMPERMANENCE

Nothing lasts forever. The world is in constant flux. In this universe, frogs and salmon are spawning their eggs at the same time that ancient stars are collapsing and new ones emerging. Great cliffs are worn away by the ocean, continents shift on tectonic plates, entire beaches can get carried off and then deposited on the other side of the world. Mighty buildings fall into disrepair when unmaintained, and great wounds heal in time. Philip Ardagh once said, half-cocked, "Time is a great healer… it also gives you the opportunity to bleed" (Ardagh, 2008).

The idea to focus on is that nothing is permanent, things are constantly changing, including our state of wellbeing. Whether it's for better or worse, nothing stays as it is. In a materialist society, focused on accumulating vast stocks of things, people often inadvertently train their minds to see the world as permanent, static, unchanging. However, permanence is merely an ideal that exists only in frozen images or perfect imaginary futures. Permanence does not exist in the present, because when we open our eyes we see new things happening all the time. Even the skin cells on your fingertips are being born and dying at a phenomenal rate. Change, then, is our only constant.

But what does this mean in terms of our grief? Does it mean we shouldn't grieve? Of course not! We have every right to mourn our losses! What impermanence teaches us, however, is that the future is never set in stone and that we aren't perfect, godlike beings with the power to perfectly control outcomes all the time. It also teaches us that *we* aren't as set in stone as we think either. This encourages us to be more mindful of what is happening to us and around us right now, and gives us the freedom to redefine who we are according to our present circumstances rather than who we thought we once were, or who we think we should be. Of course, our actions in the present can influence what happens in the future, but the present is where our true control lies.

What impermanence also teaches us is that our grief won't be the same from day to day either. When we try to imagine a future with our grief, we tend to see it as dark and unending, whereas the truth isn't so bleak. What is true, however, is that we feel dark and unending *now*. But maybe we'll feel okay tomorrow. One day, we might even smile. But then, maybe the very next day, our grief will be back and it'll hurt like hell.

When we accept that our grief isn't a constant in life, but rather an aspect of our present that rises and falls like the ocean, it becomes a little less scary. Thanks to the triggering of the "avoidance" parts of our brain, especially in complicated grief, we often want to try to dance around our own pain, to ignore it, as a way to move on with life. But again, our grief is impermanent. It will come and go as it pleases, regardless of our constant wishes, until it can resolve itself. The best way to work through grief then is not by trying to run away from it, but rather from acknowledging it when we feel its presence, and then *permitting it to leave*. This is gentler than the commonly-held belief that grief must be evicted, as well as being more effective in the sense that this softer stance tends to prevent internal conflicts. Although you may suffer, at least you won't be tearing yourself apart as well. Your grief deserves your attention on its own, it does not need to be partnered with more pains.

Of course, I do not mean to imply that you're running from your own grief in that last paragraph, but such an idea was something I have been tempted by myself, so I wished to assure you that there are other ways through this.

Most of us, I feel, will find it easy to acknowledge our grief when it manifests in us. Usually, the difficulty is in gaining a deeper under-standing, or in getting others to acknowledge our pain with us. The greatest difficulty, however, is in letting go. So, how do we do this? Why should we?

LETTING GO

What does it mean to let go? From Chapter 1, you may still remember that it does not mean letting go of memories. It does not mean letting go of love. It means letting go of mental clutter and clearing away distractions, just like before.

Let me show you.

Return back to your meditation position, in your light and dry sitting area. Make sure your spine is supporting your body. This time, place a greater focus on your breathing. Instead of placing your hand on your heart, place it just above your belly button. If you can feel any tension in your muscles, let that tension go but keep your hand where it is. Additionally, make each breath as deep as you can, exercising your diaphragm. Count each of your exhalations as you go. Now, we are primed to let go. The practice of letting go is actually quite easy, and isn't as extreme as one might think. All you need to do is be aware of your thoughts; our minds love to wander, especially when we're breathing or counting. These thoughts could be related to your grief, or they could be related to something unrelated, like your socks.

However, once you grab onto any subject in your mind, your thoughts may begin to spiral. Do I have enough clothes in my cupboard for the coming season? Did I remember to pick up fresh socks to replace the ones that got all those holes in them? Oh, hang on, I'm wearing sandals this month so it shouldn't matter anyway. But wait a second, what if so and so pulls through and they end up making plans for us to cycle together this weekend? Do my cycling shoes still fit me?

Your thoughts, once a subject is in mind, can run potentially forever. Letting go, in the context of grief, simply means recognizing when your thoughts are about to enter a spiral and then, very gently, bringing your focus back to the counting of your breath. The more you practice this, the better you'll become at noticing when your thoughts are spiraling. The better you become at noticing this, the better you'll be at bringing your mind back to a point of focus and concentration. Eventually, you won't even need to meditate to do this; you'll be able to bring your thoughts back to a neutral starting point from anywhere.

This is how you let go. Your grief will never be gone but, by developing a will to return your mind to a neutral point instead of getting lost in a spiral, you will become the master of your pain, rather than letting your pain become the master of you. This "neutral point" may still feel bittersweet, or tinged with sadness for a while. This is alright. The important thing is that you're able to step back mentally when what you're experiencing begins to spiral into a sensation that feels insurmountable. When you let go and reset for a second, you give yourself a second chance to look at your experience. When you do this, continuing with a meaningful life begins to seem more possible again.

This is because you're giving yourself space to deal with your grief on your own terms. Your grief may seem to come and go according to its own will, but by being able to notice its presence and bring your thoughts back to pace accordingly, you give yourself the ability to tell your grief, "Okay, I think I see what you're saying, but please slow down and start over."

Cutting our spirals short helps us spot what's hurting us most, and from there helps us decide when and how best to address our emotional wounds.

MINDFULNESS

Nothing is permanent. Your emotions, especially, aren't unchanging entities. They aren't absolutes either. Grief is not good. Grief is not bad. Anger is not good. Anger is not bad. It all depends on the context and how you choose to act on what you feel. Even love can become abusive or possessive when it is not matured with compassion, and even compassion can be misleading from time to time when used without experience.

Does this mean it's best to then suppress our emotions so that we never make mistakes or feel pain? Of course not.

Growing up without pains or mistakes is impossible, and grief is not the only thing you are permitted to feel during this time. A nasty side effect of early attempts to suppress or avoid our grief is that we often end up suppressing many of our other emotions too; they all flow through the same medium, after all. Accidentally suppressing your thoughts can stunt your ability to deal with grief, and may even lead to depression. Suppressing thoughts or feelings can also prevent valuable growth from taking place.

For instance, maybe deep down you felt relieved when someone you loved died. Normally, the thought is unthinkable. But what if you'd watched them suffer in great pain fighting illness for the past few months? As sad as you were to see them go, part of you is happy that at least they've found peace. There is no shame in this. Seemingly contrasting feelings are allowed to coexist with one another.

Some people even have the urge to laugh after they've experienced a deep loss because as depressing and senseless as life can be, it is equally absurd. These feelings are often difficult to talk about with those close to us because it's very easy for our words to come out the wrong way. "I'm happy he died," never sounds good, no matter what the actual meaning or intention was. This is partially why I recommended journaling earlier; it helps you discuss things that no one else can really understand. It's also why I recommend meditation to you; it helps you catch thoughts that might at first seem overwhelming or confounding.

It took me a while to realize but, eventually, I learned that the intensity of my grief actually has very little correlation with how much I loved my mother while she was alive. This was difficult to spot at first, because I loved her very much, but also grieved very much as well. It was only as I gradually let go of this pain while holding onto her memory that I began to learn this lesson. It was only as the sadness became distant while my love remained close that I understood. This annoyed me a little, because it would've been a handy thing to know earlier. No matter.

Mindfulness and meditation are important because one's culture isn't a one-size-fits-all solution to how we deal with grief. The point is, giving ourselves time for self-reflection is vital for personal resolution. If we depend too much on outside sources, then we have too many people telling us it is time to move on, or get over it, as though grief was nothing but a 5-foot fence.

Everyone grieves at their own pace. Even now, I still have moments where I cry from my past grief. I look at what I've gone on to accomplish in my personal life, and it makes me sad to think my mother will never see it, or that I'll never know for sure if she sees it.

Grief, particularly grief from death, is one of the most difficult things to live through. Breaking my arm, burning my hand, or even getting sand shot into my eye didn't hurt anywhere near as much. Even acknowledging that you're on one of the most difficult paths of your life can be reassuring. If meditation gives you mindfulness and mastery over this, then you can gain mindfulness or mastery over anything.

5

SLEEP BETTER

HOW GRIEF AFFECTS SLEEP

W hen we first lose someone important to us, sleep can feel nearly impossible. Our bodies are wired to stay awake during times of stress, and this includes the intense anxiety of compli- cated grief as well as the low hum of depression.

Though you might be lucky enough to have avoided developing complicated grief, 25% of people who experience bereavement from losing a romantic or marriage partner end up developing clinical depression within the first year of their loss, making sleep even harder.

Even if you are fortunate enough to be part of the remaining 75%, basic grief also comes with trauma that leads to disruptive physical symptoms that can last for months. This in turn can lead to insomnia, even in cases where complicated grief does not develop (Tuck Sleep, 2020).

Common barriers to a restful sleep are constant thoughts of loss, which keeps us stressed especially if we haven't been regularly journaling or exercising. In cases where sleep is achieved, it's still possible to wake up feeling a new intensity of bereavement after dreaming about one's lost loved one. Such dreams are commonly a way for our subconscious minds to process the grief on an emotional level, so do not worry if you are experiencing them; it is a sign that your body is trying to heal itself. It's also a clear sign that you need to give yourself more time to process your trauma.

There is nothing wrong with thinking or dreaming about a lost loved one. However, when we dwell on these thoughts obsessively to the point of losing sleep, we begin to enter a vicious circle.

Sleep deprivation occurs either when we're getting substantially fewer hours of sleep than we're used to, or when we're getting the same–or even more–hours but at a wildly inconsistent pace. Sleep deprivation, in turn, makes us more susceptible to illness as well as reduces our ability to cope with stress and anxiety. This vulnerability to stress and anxiety makes it harder for us to meditate, harder for us to process our grief and harder for us to accurately recall information, harming our ability to think and make effective decisions.

All these issues can then increase the severity of our grief, making it even *harder* for us to sleep, increasing the severity of our sleep deprivation and beginning the grief-intensifying cycle all over again. To get the most out of the previous 4 habits, then, we need to pay special attention to our sleep.

In contrast, how does good sleep affect grief? To start, a good night's sleep significantly reduces the odds of developing complicated grief or depression further down the line and makes any existing depression or complicated grief easier to deal with. A good sleep makes it easier for us to keep our heads clear and deal with our pain on our own terms, but on a more foundational level than meditation. Good sleep is a force multiplier for all your other coping mechanisms and grief-processing habits.

HOW MUCH PRIORITY SHOULD YOU PLACE ON SLEEP?

Many of us make the mistake of thinking sleep isn't important, while some of us simply feel too busy to prioritize it much. As a result, perhaps you wish to puzzle out how big of a difference some extra attention to your sleep will make for you.

Several scientific studies have been carried out to demonstrate how important observation of proper sleep routines are for grievers, especially if they're widows or widowers. Psychiatry research published by Elsevier uncovered that you're 4 times more likely to suffer from sleep deprivation than normal while grieving. This was discovered when 100% of all widow participants were found to suffer from poor sleep compared to only 25% of all non-bereaved participants. If you've lost someone, then, poor sleep may certainly be making things harder than you'd expect (Pasternak *et al*, 1992).

Another study published by Elsevier in 1996 further uncovered that deeper feelings of grief led to more serious levels of sleep deprivation, in line with our earlier idea of sleep deprivation and bereavement forming a vicious circle (Brown *et al*).

For women, the issue can be even worse as both menstruation and menopause can lead to sleep-disrupting changes in body chemistry. It can be especially difficult for older women, as the decreased production of estrogen and progesterone in the Autumn months already leads to risks of depression and sleep loss before grief is even factored in (Tuck Sleep, 2020c).

So, if you are approaching middle-age, are grieving over a death, or are female, then resolving your sleep could lead to a massive improvement to your overall wellbeing.

However, it doesn't stop there; don't think you can ignore sleep just because you're young or male. In a study conducted by Research Gate in 2005, observations of over 800 college students of various ages and genders found that those in mourning exhibited more severe degrees of insomnia and impaired cognition, with the common barriers mentioned earlier being the biggest reasons.

The European Respiratory Journal also found that in cases where the loss was the death of a family member in intensive care, the chances of developing complicated grief rose from 25% to 50%, additionally increasing the chance of poor sleep and the beginning of a truly vicious cycle.

In other words, the more personal your loss, and the more deeply you feel it, the more deeply you'll benefit from giving care to your sleep cycle. However, everyone who grieves will suffer from poor sleep to some degree, and can thus still benefit from the advice below.

CREATING AN IDEAL SLEEP SCHEDULE

When we're grieving, we already feel overwhelmed. Certainly, the thought of sorting out our sleep schedule isn't likely to cross our mind and, even if it does, how do we start?

The golden rule is consistency. If you've ever heard stories of people achieving great success on very little sleep, your jaw may have hit the floor. "How on Earth do they do it?" you may have asked. The trick is consistency. Most people are comfortable with 7-8 hours of sleep per night, although some can run on 6 while others need 10-12. Regardless of how much you need, setting a schedule to both go to bed and to wake up at the same time every day, even on weekends, already kicks you off to a good start. The longer you keep to these times, the easier they'll be to live by, and the better you'll feel. So, right now, go ahead and set a sleep and wake-up time for yourself that you're comfortable with. As with all things, don't be afraid to take baby steps. You don't want your sleep/wake times to be more than an hour more or less than what you're used to. If you want, choose something based on the schedule you had before your grief.

Now that you've decided on a time, you might be asking, "Well, how do I make sure I will stick to this? What if my body doesn't want to sleep when I do? What if my thoughts are too difficult to sleep through?"

Luckily, there are ways to cope and retake control of your rest.

The first thing you may wish to do is cut naps out of your schedule. An afternoon siesta is fine if you're used to it, but for most people, naps only make it harder for them to get the sleep they need at night. To avoid this, it is recommended that you keep your naps no longer than 30 minutes; it can be quite difficult to wake from a sleep that goes on longer than half an hour. If you absolutely must sleep longer than that time, make it no longer than one hour, and set an alarm to make sure you'll get up when you need to.

However, naps aren't exactly our biggest worries, are they? After all, the common barriers to a good rest are tortured dreams and thoughts of loss, not siestas. To help remind yourself that you are not alone, and that you do have love and support should you need it, consider reaching out to a friend or family member. Invite them to spend time with you, and even invite them to spend the night if you'd like. If friends or family aren't available, letting a pet comfort you can also be effective. If you shared a bed with your loved one before your loss, consider sleeping on their side of the bed. You might find it comforting, if still bittersweet, and it might be easier to sleep when you're not constantly looking at the empty space they used to occupy. It might be easier to look at your own empty space. A body pillow can help even further; body pillows not only support your muscles and help them relax, the feeling of holding onto something soft can help your body and mind wind down just enough to get a healthy sleep. The pillow won't replace your lost loved one, of course, but that's not the point of the pillow; the pillow is just there to help you maintain your physical and mental health during a trying time.

The next best thing to do is cut alcohol or sleeping pills out of your pre-bed ritual. While they can be handy for enforcing consistency in your sleep, they don't allow for very deep sleeps, and can even give you terrible bouts of anxiety while you're unconscious, severely limiting your rest quality and causing feelings of fatigue regardless of how many hours you were knocked out. If you absolutely need a sleeping aid, ask your doctor about melatonin supplements. Melatonin is a natural hormone produced by your body when you're in dark or dimly lit areas. The more melatonin in your system at once, the drowsier you become. This hormone is what usually lets us fall asleep, but it's quite common for its natural synthesis to be disrupted by great stress after a loss.

In these cases, getting melatonin can be quite helpful for getting your sleeping cycle back on track, but there are natural alternatives to help bring your melatonin production back to a healthy schedule.

THE NATURAL WAYS

Let's start with the low-hanging fruit; caffeine is not recommended after lunchtime. Caffeine's wakefulness effects can last up to 6 hours after you drink it, and its alertness boost does not necessarily increase awareness; rather, it makes you more anxious and twitchy. Coffee is an obvious source, but most sodas and colas have this issue, as well as some teas and many forms of hot chocolate. Consider these drinks "comfort food," as per Chapter 2. These may have been fine for you in the past when you didn't have grief to contend with, but the wakefulness brought by these drinks is too much when dealing with bereavement simultaneously. Keep these drinks for the morning and afternoon, and stick to water in the evening. Small amounts at night are still fine, but only if you're confident you'll still be able to sleep well. If you aren't sleeping well, these drinks may be a contributing factor to your frustration.

Other than that, the dietary recommendations given in Chapter 2 will already help you achieve more peaceful sleep at night. If you need a little extra help, increase your intake of oats, bananas, tomatoes, walnuts or cherries during dinners or desserts, all of which are rich in natural melatonin.

If you want to boost your body's melatonin production rather than relying on foods already containing it, however, then you may prefer foods rich in vitamin B6. Vitamin B6 helps your nervous system send signals properly throughout your body. This will not only improve your body's ability to produce melatonin when it is needed, but it may also have an added effect of helping you process what's around you and find greater calmness as a result.

Foods rich in B6 include pistachio nuts, bananas, raw garlic, chickpeas and fish. Out of the fish, halibut and tuna are some of the richest in B6, as is salmon.

Aside from your diet, you can also improve your sleep every night through controlling the lights in your house. Remember, melatonin is produced in dim light and darkness. Leaving your lights on, then, just encourages you to stay awake longer.

Note that, although the yellow lights of your house may be the most obviously bright light sources around you, your phone and computer screens are actually much worse. Although they won't brightly light up a room the same way a bulb does, the light emitted by screens tends to be based on blue light. Blue light is by far the most intense kind of visible light, and as such stimulates your brain far more than the yellow light of your bulbs. This stimulation can encourage you to stay awake even after the blue light has been blocked or turned off and, for this reason, it is best if you avoid phone and computer screens as much as possible about an hour before you intend to sleep.

Beyond our body's physical response to screen light encouraging us to stay awake, screens tend to show us a host of mental stimulants that keep us up too; social media is readily addictive and stimulating in its random reward system. Dramatic, explicit or unnerving content can also keep our brain ticking for hours after we turn our screens off, making sleep difficult after watching a horror movie or emotional TV drama. Avoiding these kinds of shows and content for at least an hour before bed can help you get a restful sleep without cutting these things out of your life entirely.

Finally, our digital media can be full of reminders of our loss, which can raise anxiety and encourage unhelpful rumination if we aren't journaling. Of course, it's a bad idea to avoid these things entirely; simply give yourself time to deal with them earlier in the day so that you can leave your nights open to soak in your melatonin and drift off to sleep.

TURN YOUR BEDROOM INTO A SANCTUARY OF SLEEP

Aside from diet and darkness, there are additional ways to gently transform your bedroom into a more comfortable place to sleep. Part of this lies in how you treat your bedroom.

The first thing you may wish to do is locate any reminders of your loved one, like photographs, books or clothing. Although these objects can trigger grief, it's important to spend a little time with them so you can decide what to do with them. If you've been battling to sleep due to grief, consider moving these items to other parts of your house, such as your living room. As a general rule, it's a good idea to keep anything not associated with sleep or sex outside of your bedroom; this will make it easier for your brain to associate your room with sleep and thus get into the correct mood for deep rest. Moving objects associated with your lost loved one to other parts of the house, then, can tell your brain that it's okay to set aside grief at least a little bit in order to achieve a good night's rest. Decluttering other objects like electronics, toys or excess items can further help your brain focus on sleep, even if the items have very little to do with your loved one. You can make the relocation of these items temporary, or until you feel your grief is manageable again. Alternatively, you can choose to relocate these items permanently. It is up to you.

If you have the energy to redecorate your room entirely, strongly consider using shades of blue, which tend to evoke feelings of calm and hope. Even if all feels lost, hope remains a useful tool for overcoming psychologically stressful situations. If your bedroom isn't a quiet place, consider playing electronically recorded sounds taken from nature as ambient noise. Although noise typically disrupts sleep, constant sounds like the wind, the ocean or crickets chirping can loop back to being soothing. Disruptive sounds can ruin our sleep quality even while we're dreaming, but soothing ambiance or complete silence can let us get the quality rest we need during grief.

Another thing you can try to help get into the right mindset for sleeping in your bedroom is the development of a bed-time routine. Pick something you'd be comfortable doing every day about 1 hour or less before bed. An obvious one is to start dimming or even turning off the lights inside your house, and making sure all your curtains are firmly shut, so that it's dark enough for your body to ramp up the melatonin production.

A warm bath or cup of caffeine-free tea (such as herbal or chamomile) are also great ways to help your body relax physically, making sleep an easier prospect. If you find it difficult to get off your electronic devices, despite knowing how bad they are for your sleep, consider writing letters or reading a book instead as a way to unwind without exposing yourself to blue light. Finally, consider meditating before bed, just like how we described in Chapter 4. Meditation will allow you to bring today's grief forward and deal with it compassionately, allowing you to resolve some of your pains so you don't carry them all to bed.

SYNERGIZING EXERCISE AND JOURNALING WITH SLEEP

Meditation and diet aren't the only tips that synergize with your sleep. When grieving, it is not uncommon to experience restlessness. When waking up in the middle of the night, do not stress, and do not begin watching your clock. Clock-watching is a notorious stressor, and as such will only make it more difficult for you to return to sleep. Rather, if you've woken up, the best thing you can do is just try to fall asleep again, without stressing over how much time it feels like it's taking. Our perception of time isn't always accurate in the middle of the night. Count to 600 while you wait. If you get to 601 and still don't feel sleepy, get up, grab your journal, move into another room and spend a little time writing about your thoughts. Writing about what's bothering you can help you process it just enough so you can comfortably return to bed again.

You are welcome to re-enact your bedtime routine of tea, bathing or reading again if you wish, and then once again return to bed. Giving yourself some time to unwind in this way during a restless night can help you make the most of what time you have left.

Exercising in the evening after you are finished with work can also help tire your body out further and put it in the mood to rest, which can help with sleep. Do not do this less than an hour or two before bed, however, as the energy activated by your exercise will need some time to cool off before its drowsiness effect will kick in. If you have less than 60 minutes before bed, or if you've woken up in the middle of the night, it is better to stretch than to perform full-on exercises so that you avoid activating your energy stores, which could potentially keep you up much longer than you intended if timed poorly.

6

UPDATE YOUR BRAIN

In Chapter 2, I compared the human brain to a computer and stated that water was the coolant needed to keep it running optimally. So far, we've largely been dealing with "hardware": how to take care of your body, and how to reduce physical and emotional stress on a mechanical level. However, your hardware is only one side of boosting performance. To run as best you can, you also need updated software.

Software updates help eliminate bugs or block viruses. Likewise, updating your brain helps you spot limiting beliefs, remove logical fallacies and block misleading or self-destructive thoughts.

But how do we update our brains? By reading, of course!

If you've been struggling to make time for reading, choose a book on something you enjoy; books these days cover everything from culture, science and religion to fantasy, comedy and legend. Once you've chosen something compelling, make a point of reading anywhere between 1-40 pages from that book each night as part of your pre-bed routine. If you use public transport, another great reading spot is on the bus or train. Finally, if you're so absolutely busy that neither of those options is viable, at least keep it for your lunch breaks. Some people speak as if TV and books are mutually exclusive, but this does not need to be true.

But, thanks to the benefits, it's recommended you fit reading at least somewhere in your life. If I've done my job, you've already updated your brain several times as a result of what you've read so far. Just like journaling, reading is a powerful self-education tool that can empower you through opening new doors and considering new perspectives.

EMPATHY AND PERSPECTIVE

Speaking of perspective, reading is a doorway into the minds of other people. This means that the stereotype of the arrogant and insufferable bookwork is not inherently true; while reading very narrowly can cause tensions, it is also true that reading widely allows you to broaden your mind and, through understanding, become a more compassionate person. By reading this book, for instance, you have been given a key into parts of my mind, and through that the opportunity to grow closer to me as a person, even though we may have never met. We all live through our personal narratives and have our view of the world subjectively distorted through our experiences, and allowing me to share mine with you is a treasure that benefits us both.

However, no single person's experiences lend a complete view of life. Reading is what lets us see into the minds, motivations, insights and value systems of people from other cultures, faiths, age groups, gender identities, sexualities, economic classes, and more. Reading, then, is not just a source of knowledge and ideas, it is also a way for us to understand other people in this world. Reading also gives us the rare gift of allowing us to see into people's minds across centuries. Even in a world where nothing is permanent, what a person writes tends to outlive the person themselves, giving us insights into how humans from a variety of cultures lived, spoke and thought.

When we're grieving, reading about someone else's trials and tribulations can sometimes feel like the last thing we want, and yet it's those alternate perspectives that we come to crave when we feel lost. After all, that's why you're here, isn't it? Whether a book is fictional or not, reading about another person's experiences and how they overcome the obstacles in their life is, when written well, inspiring. It makes our own obstacles seem more possible. An uphill battle that once seemed hopeless now looks winnable. The best fantasy and science fiction works not because it's full of wizards or space-giants or enchanted laser swords. The best science fiction and fantasy stories work because the main characters are still relatable on a very grounded level, and their ability to learn about, navigate and cope in such a strange world is encouraging. Real life itself is quite strange, too.

As difficult as it was for me to lose my mother in such a short amount of time, Joan Didion's *The Year Of Magical Thinking* gave me solace and perspective; she'd lost her husband at the same time that her daughter was in a coma, and she dives into the events in a raw biography of beauty and pain. Reading it inspired me to soldier on and find new hope. Any genre in both fictional and non-fictional storytelling can help with grief if it is sensitive, observant and well-written. Never forget that.

Reading widely, from authors of many different viewpoints and creeds, will let you inhabit multiple perspectives at a time. This way of seeing things will make it easier for you to understand multiple angles on any given issue, but also the thought processes of those around you. The more thought processes you encounter through reading, the more likely you are to respond compassionately to the thought processes of others, because you'll be more likely to relate them to an author or character you familiarized yourself with in the past.

This in turn can lead to you forming more deep and complex relationships, as long as you recognize that a person is more than the thought processes they choose to show; who they remind you of isn't all they are, by any means. But being able to engage with what they present to you on their surface is what will help you engage more deeply further down the line. This can reduce loneliness, strengthen existing connections, and give you a powerful web of support in times of grief. Empathy is one of the most powerful social skills on Earth, and mind-reading is one of the most awesome superpowers. Reading widely and frequently will help you develop the first, and get awfully close to mimicking the second.

Finally, reading can cut down your insomnia by half, dramatically increasing the quality of your rest and, consequently, reducing the odds of lashing out or being irritable with those around you. This, in turn, can help you establish greater levels of empathy before even factoring your multiple perspectives into account.

STRENGTHENING INNOVATION

Being able to consider a subject from multiple perspectives isn't just to improve empathy or simulate mind-reading, however. When you constantly expose yourself to the ideas of other people, you begin to see patterns and form connections between their work that allows you to develop their thoughts along a path that even they might never have expected. This is how inventions and advancements are made. Being familiar with one person's work will only let you understand that specific artist, but being familiar with many people's works and seeing where they could potentially support each other can let you create something novel and new. We are not finished inventing everything yet; most of us simply don't read enough to conceive of anything new.

And that is just in the context of non-fiction. In the realms of fiction, a good book will encourage us to visualize detailed characters and grand vistas in our minds. Unlike films, which tend to spoon-feed us both audibly and visually, books let our imaginations become virtually limitless in the way we interpret words and shift their contexts. Reading, then, turns you into your own virtual film-maker, crafting dozens or even scores of different scenes rolling in your mind, possibly all focused around a single paragraph.

This encouragement of the imagination is good for your brain for reasons similar to why journaling is; it makes you an active interpreter and creator who is involved in the information being presented. Any piece of media that succeeds at this is brilliant, but books are encouraged the most to get this aspect right. A film or video-game can afford to cut their budget on the writing if the visuals, mechanics or acting are good enough, but a book cannot afford a cop-out like that. Writing is all a book has, and for this reason, a greater proportion of published books are likely to contain ideas primed to spark your creative side compared to the number of published films or games.

If you ever feel stuck or unsure what to do next, reading multiple books on the subject will invariably inspire you and give you more creative wiggle room to achieve the kind of life you want.

And, as you read, you'll begin to realize more and more how little any of us truly know. The more you read the more you'll naturally want to make time for reading, as your thirst for knowledge will only grow. This knowledge will continue to empower you in unexpected ways, in turn. Intelligence isn't something we're just born with, it's something we earn through experience; a person who doesn't read will only ever have their own experiences, but the person who reads and forms connections between everything they learn will accrue the experience of a thousand lifetimes, and consequently endow themselves with a wisdom that far surpasses their years. If you're worried about becoming haughty in your knowledge, simply remember that what you learned did not start with you; what you have is a gift that's been built on by people around the world across chasms of time.

ANALYTICAL THINKING

The benefits of reading do not just end at vicariously living multiple lives or benefitting from the enhanced generation of ideas, however. Reading not only stimulates the creative side of your brain, but encourages your logical side too. While you can analyze any book, including fictional ones if they're well-written, Western Nonfiction books especially present us with a body of information that was structured with intention in a specific order. Getting into the habit of critically analyzing the order that books present their information in, and even challenging the established order through seeing where else a paragraph or chapter could fit, will greatly enhance your ability to organize information rationally. After doing this with many books, the process will become quick, easy and natural.

You can take this a step further by trying to map out a summary of the book's narrative on one page. Schools tend to make the process feel boring and dry, but it's actually a wonderful way of taking your depth of analysis to the next level, as spotting and ordering narrative elements according to your own observations can help you pick up patterns you may have missed. You might even spot arcs and themes you'd missed before. Just bear in mind that almost anything can be made a theme with enough creativity; logical analysis, however, is what lets you consider the merit of a theme beyond its premise.

In the modern-day, you can take your analysis even further by using websites like TVTropes, which tend to be amazing starting points for those who want to broaden their analysis or spot overlooked threads in a story. Although, in the same way that a book club won't necessarily help you write a book, sites and forums similar to TVTropes can only encourage a certain form of logical analysis; it's good for breaking down a piece of work. Creating a work, however, requires imagination (see previous section).

FORMING CONNECTIONS

Becoming knowledgeable of alternate perspectives and building empathy already helps one with forming connections, but what are the other ways in which writing aids such endeavors? After all, surely it isn't possible to read a book by every sort of person on Earth? How can reading possibly help with forming connections on a universal level?

Even if you do not understand a particular person's point of view, being a widely-read individual at least increases the chance of there being some common ground or overlap.

When you have read the same book as another person, you immediately have a strong building-point for a friendship. This person can then provide you their perspective in a fun manner if you then decide to unpack the book's contents together. I do this with one of my best friend's, and the conversations we have are some of the most in-depth I've had in my life, I'm sure he'd say the same.

But even if the people you're dealing with have not read the same books as you, and you do not understand their perspectives, your expanded vocabulary gained through reading can increase the chances of them understanding yours. The more words you know, the more easily you'll be able to approach a topic verbally while achieving the result you want. A great example of this is Desdemona's speech to her father in *Othello*, where her use of wordplay allows her to communicate her love for Othello without denouncing or estranging her father. The better our grasp of language and the better our understanding of a word's colloquial use, the better positioned we are to combine context as well as language content to communicate vivid messages. One of Terry Pratchett's great strengths as a writer was his ability to place normally unrelated words alongside one another in ways that people could still readily understand and even appreciate. Being an avid reader improves one's ability to do this through writing, and with a little practice, through speech, with poetry being the logical conclusion of this practice… even though poetry seems to be a somewhat esoteric art in the modern age.

This expanded vocabulary is better for more than just sounding clever or having a wider toolbelt for your verbal communication, however. A heightened understanding of your language, combined with enhanced analytical, creative, and personal empathic skills, can make you an extremely interesting person. That's not to say you aren't interesting already, of course, but sharpening both halves of your brain as well as improving your ability to communicate can help others *see and hear* how interesting you truly are. Not everyone will be interested in the same things of course, but spending time reading what you care about each day will help you come across as more interesting to the kind of people you'd want to hang out with.

Maybe you felt mildly offended when I mentioned the halves of the brain, and believe that the divisions are much more complex than one half being logical and one half being creative. Well, by being well-read on the subject you could launch into a highly-detailed, informative and superlatively interesting discussion on the matter; a discussion you might balk, hesitate or stumble over if you hadn't read enough to feel sure of what you're saying.

And that's another thing; reading makes you more confident in specific areas of knowledge. You might still feel scared, unsure or otherwise lost when it comes to subjects you're not familiar with. A stereotypical computer geek, for instance, might still feel a little uneasy talking about football. But that same geek will be able to reveal an entire world in the micrometer-thick lattices that splay in geometric patterns across your motherboard.

Being able to boast immense self-confidence on certain subjects due to a mixture of knowledge and experience is empowering, although one should never forget that knowledge doesn't just come from books, it comes from people too. When making a real-life comparison to someone who has a mixture of knowledge, I think of Joe Rogan. Listening to his podcasts and the wide variety of guests he has on the show, he asks very thought-provoking questions, while giving his own viewpoint. His ability to hold long conversations with people from completely opposite industries is what makes his show so impressive and popular.

7

CONFIDE

Sometimes, confiding in another person is one of the hardest things we can do. We all want to share our pains with someone close to us, someone who understands, yet often we're held back by fears or disappointment. Maybe the person we're speaking to doesn't understand. Maybe they do, but we feel like we're being a burden. Or maybe there's something we desperately want to get off our chests, and yet we do not have the words. Maybe we just don't feel ready to properly confront what we're going through, even though we feel ready to talk about it. These feelings are all normal; that means as painful as they are, you aren't alone in your experience of them.

The last six chapters were all devoted to helping you take the best care of yourself possible so that the need to confide wouldn't be as strong. In the case of Chapters 3 and 6, you were given ways to help you express your thoughts to those around you without making yourself dependent on their responses.

Now, however, you are ready to start reaching out to others if you haven't already. If you don't feel ready yet, that's alright; you must go at your own pace. Simply know that you're already armed with everything you need to confide in another person once again.

However, friends and family won't always be the people you wish to confide in. While they generally mean well and have your best interests at heart, they also have their own fears and pains to worry about, which means that you might not be able to have as much of their attention as you would like.

If you're ready to confide and yet still feel lonely or unheard despite speaking up, the best thing you can do is seek professional help. Media stereotypes like to portray professional help as a shameful last resort only taken when there is no other choice. This, however, is only because sitcoms with functional individuals aren't as interesting as TV shows where everything is dramatic and blown out of proportion.

Professional help isn't a sign of trouble, or an admission of defeat. Therapists, after all, are simply human beings like you and I. There is no shame in speaking to one. The biggest difference between them and us is that they devote their entire life to helping people conquer grief, overcome fear and achieve resolutions for complex decisions.

It doesn't matter if the troubles are big or small, they are there to listen to you and guide you towards making decisions that ultimately benefit you. Unlike friends or family, who can have their attention divided by their jobs, for therapists this care *is* their job. This, along with professional training in empathy and communication, makes them perfect for helping you scratch long-term psychological itches; family and friends will touch your heart and lift your spirits, but therapists are vital for helping you make psychological breakthroughs that multiply the effectiveness of any compassion shown by your loved ones. For this reason, therapists should not be eschewed. They're like an omnibus of information relevant to your neuroses, so why not pay to read one?

Compare them to dentists; you don't wait until a tooth needs to be pulled before you go and see them, although they certainly are helpful for that. Rather, you visit them somewhat regularly, even if it's just twice a year, and incorporate their advice into your life as much as healthily possible. Likewise, professional therapy is useful even when nothing is particularly wrong. For instance, professional counseling can help reduce the physical harm caused by stress even further, as well as reconnect with your earlier passions maturely.

This reconnection is important, as a lot of what made us special as children is tarnished as we form a series of defense mechanisms in an attempt to protect ourselves from fear, hurt, trouble or any number of suppressive emotions. Therapists have a talent for deftly pointing out recurring thought patterns that may be holding us back in this way, and can help us drop the behaviors that no longer serve our own best interests.

Self-destructive behavior can be subtle, but having it be revealed to oneself can help us escape perpetual feelings of persecution, victimization and powerlessness. Even if we live in a reality where we are persecuted, victimized or disempowered, the insights of a therapist can allow you to find fonts of hidden strength within yourself, and from there help you empower yourself and perhaps even change the reality you live in.

REDEFINE UNHEALTHY PATTERNS

You already have the power to redefine some of your less healthy or grief-amplifying habits, if you have any. Maybe exercise has made it easier for you to cut down on alcohol. Maybe journaling or reading has helped you cut down on other grief-amplifiers, like gluttony or sugar. Certainly, a reading habit is one of the most healthy habits you can have, as binging a book in a moment of weakness is significantly healthier than satisfying that weakness with a cigarettes, a bottle of liquor, or a week's supply of doughnuts.

You already have the power to sort out much of your own confusion and turmoil but, even so, a therapist can be a welcome companion. The habits from the previous chapters allow you to approach your counselor from a position of relative strength, but that doesn't mean you need to pretend as if you have no vulnerabilities at all.

Expressing yourself openly and honestly to someone knowledgeable in the science of therapy can lead to unexpected revelations. One such man, named Eric Hotchandani, found that most of his clients experience a sort of mid-decade crisis every 10 years, where they feel as though they aren't active participants in their own lives. This can lead to expressions of dissatisfaction with relationships, or even their lives as a whole.

According to Eric, this dissatisfaction with life or relations often doesn't have much to do with the relations themselves. According to him, it mostly comes from the common Western practice of filling our houses and lives with objects that aren't personally fulfilling (Tartakovsky, 2019). This doesn't mean that one needs to become a full-blown minimalist to be happy, of course, but he does have a point. By filling our houses with things that don't add value to our lives, we rob ourselves of space and force ourselves into a claustrophobic living environment that leaves us unhappy without adding any corresponding benefit. Living in a dirty or cluttered space can be stressful, and stress, in turn, can exacerbate grief or depression. It's difficult to feel calm when we feel like we're going to be buried under the weight of everything around us.

Even emotional clutter, like the constant belief that we need to be perfect and successful all the time, can be sources of stress that lead to dissatisfaction, even when what we already have is rather good.

When we choose to fill our lives with objects or ideals that do not match our true beliefs or active goals, we end up over-complicating our identities as well as our sense of purpose. In the same way that loss can upset our sense of self, so can possession.

If you aren't a big reader, for instance, owning multiple bookshelves crammed with knowledge that you'll never read can confuse your identity and make you feel like a fraud, even though in reality you may be a deeply intelligent individual thanks to prior learning or strong empathy.

When we continue to keep objects in our lives that aren't in line with who we are, those feelings of confusion begin to become habits. These habits, in turn, become thought patterns that can quickly grow to become a part of one's personality. By this point, the confusion has now seeped into our very identity.

When this happens, we begin to form feelings of self-loathing, most commonly either the feeling that we deserve to live in the bad situation that we're in, or simply that we're not good enough for any of the things that we want in life. We need to remind ourselves that that's simply not true.

Despite this, such feelings invariably leak into our relationships and begin to make us psychologically harm not only ourselves, but also the people we love. Thus, it is important to have such feelings rooted out and addressed. This doesn't mean you can't accept yourself for who you are, but rather it means you are entitled to learn more about yourself and what you can bring into your life to synergize with who you are at your core. When you know how best to meet your core self in the world around you, you'll also know how best to add value back into the place you live.

RELOCATE DESIRE

Desire is not an inherently bad thing. While desire can motivate us to hurt others, or cause us to meddle in places where we shouldn't, this tends to happen when we're not thinking things through. A well-thought-out desire, on the other hand, can be a potent motive that drives us through life, such as the desire to raise a family, or the desire to master a craft.

I compared therapists to books earlier, and for good reason. A decent therapist tends to remind us that our current way of life isn't the only way that we could be living. A good therapist, like a good book, can offer us a broader perspective and deeper awareness, even though it is their empathy that carries this investigation into the self.

It's quite common for individuals to choose isolation as a response to trauma in their lives, and the reasons are ones we can readily understand; we fear opening ourselves up to give to the world only to be rejected. We fear the consequences of placing ourselves in a potentially vulnerable space where we can feel shamed or mocked. And, most of all, we deeply fear the inevitable loss that threatens us when we connect ourselves to another person.

When grieving, that fear of loss becomes fresh in our minds. When we try to share our pain with another person only for their response to brush us off (whether intentionally or not), we can feel rejected. And, most of all, we feel ashamed and mocked when people put us under constant pressure to "get over it" as if they expect our pains to run on their timetable. This shame can make us feel selfish when we are, in fact, just trying to heal from one of the most difficult experiences in our lives. I'd counter that anyone who insists that you "get over it" without actually helping you do so is being selfish themselves.

With all this in mind, it's no wonder that we might wish to isolate ourselves from everyone, especially during or after deep grief. Yet a professional therapist will quickly point out that isolation isn't the final solution for most of us; as much as we fear shame, rejection and loss, most of us also have a deep-seated need for connection.

Even the nerdiest and most anti-social among us need at least 1 or 2 high-quality friends to help brighten up their lives. Despite this, our need for intimacy, whether platonic or romantic, often does not register as a valid desire. In truth, it's one of the most valid desires a person can have. According to the Survivalist's Rule of Threes, a human needs air, water, shelter, food and *love* (The Survival Journal Editorial Staff, 2020). Remember all those funny "stranded islander" characters you'd see in kids' movies? The ones that put googly eyes on coconuts and pretended they're people? As ridiculous as that image is, it is based in truth; no one wants to feel completely alone. And if isolation goes on too long (e.g. a quarter of a year without seeing or hearing another human being at all, perhaps longer if humans are visible or audible but not interactable), the mind begins to do strange things to compensate.

While loss, shame and rejection are all forms of suffering, isolation doesn't prevent that suffering. Isolation instead has us suffer differently because while we might not know the grief of loss again, we instead begin to grieve through having a lonely heart, and the lack of contact invariably leads to chronic depression (see Chapter 1 for symptoms). A therapist can help prevent this by letting you realize and pursue your need for connection in the healthiest manner possible. Isolation does not keep you safe from anything except contagious diseases, and grief is not a disease, nor is depression contagious.

For these things, isolation is not a protective wall, nor is it a secure fortress. In fact, for psychological matters it is best compared to shutting one's eyes to block out the sun, or sticking one's head in the sand in the hope of going unnoticed by one's problems. A grief counselor, then, isn't a siege-breaker. Rather, they are a doctor with earbuds and eye drops, or a rescue serviceman prepared to gently get your head above ground again.

BUT WHAT IS GRIEF COUNSELING, EXACTLY?

As said before, therapy is for any level of grief, and while many of us are grieving from the loss of death, any form of loss can be a cause for grief. Losses such as divorce or estrangement can hit hard, even if it isn't the same thing as death. The pain of grief, meanwhile, isn't simply sadness; it can be anger too.

Therapy, or counseling, exists as both a way to promote understanding of your own grief and a way to help you avoid self-destructive psychological traps while working through your pains. This aid goes above and beyond the advice given in previous chapters, and can be a lifesaver if you were already experiencing great levels of stress or unhappiness before your loss.

A good therapist will commonly get the ball rolling by letting you talk as much as you want about your lost love; they will ask you questions to help you fill their heads with a clear image. They want to understand exactly who and what you lost. During this time, they will withhold on making any judgments and patiently allow you to talk your way through your pains.

From there, the therapist will eventually be able to identify the breaking point between the trauma of your loss and the grief of your loss. A telltale sign that you're undergoing great trauma from loss is if you have an image or memory related to the loss branded indelibly in your mind's eye. The therapist will then identify that, as long as you're undergoing trauma, you'll find processing your grief to be a constant struggle. Their goal from this point is to help soothe your trauma so you can focus on dealing with your grief appropriately. Journaling, as discussed in Chapter 3, might play a part in this, as writing about our experiences lets us bypass the circular ruminations associated with trauma. The therapist, of course, will have further tricks and skills to take this a step further. If journaling hasn't helped you, counseling may be an especially good idea for you.

Trauma usually takes sixteen sessions or more to resolve, though any of the habits you may have picked up earlier in the book can help you get through trauma faster as they help you stabilize, narrate and consolidate your experiences, all of which are needed for effective trauma dissolution.

Finally, a good therapist or counselor will help you identify your guilts and regrets. Perhaps you were skeptical earlier when I mentioned that feeling a measure of relief after a loss is not only common, but acceptable–even if those around you might not understand that. A good therapist will tell you the same thing; there's no "sadness quota" that you need to fill, and what's done is done. You cannot go back and change the past, but you can decide how you'll act going forward. A good therapist, then, will encourage you to let go of the guilt while doing the best you can to honor the memory of your lost loved ones. You could see honoring their memory as a form of atonement, but when done well, it can also become a healthy way of developing your life.

Professional therapists are incredibly well-read, highly educated individuals who deliberately train their empathy, and this leads to a curious set of behaviors. When confessing our pains to others, a common mistake non-therapists make is they open with saying "Oh well, at least <insert minor positive that resulted from a major tragedy>." Even if what they're saying is true, it isn't necessarily what you need to hear. A therapist, meanwhile, will instead respond with another, more helpful truth, "I understand what you're feeling, and I'm here to help you."

A therapist will recall their own instances of pain and grief in their lives, yet very rarely will they share them; this is because your sessions with them are about your pain, not theirs, and that's where they want to keep the focus. Instead, when they're recalling their own pains, they'll ask "What did I wish people told me when I was going through something like this?" or, "If this person is quite different from me, what's the best way for me to help them feel the way I wanted to?"

To figure these things out, a therapist will spend much more time listening to you instead of responding, in contrast to many of the people we try to talk to. They'll also offer you multiple perspectives to consider, and observe you carefully to see which ones you respond to best. For instance, the idea of the 5 Stages of Grief–Denial, Anger, Bargaining, Depression and Acceptance–is actually a severely limited way for people to process their own grief. Yet, because of how popular the format is, people end up putting a lot of pressure on themselves and feel like they're off-kilter if they skipped Bargaining, or experienced Depression both before and after Denial.

This is madness, however, and a good therapist will quickly point that out. After all, the 5 Stages *were originally intended to help individuals anticipate their own deaths.* In other words, they're designed to help people cope with a loss before it happens, but has next-to-nothing to do with processing grief after we live through experiencing a loss. A good therapist, then, will offer other ways of looking at grief-processing. Everyone's grieving format is a little different, and the therapist's ability to determine which format is best for a particular individual is what makes them so valuable.

Now, they aren't necessarily there to solve your problems directly, but they will use truth and understanding to validate how you feel so that you can process things properly yourself.

8

CHERISH POSITIVITY, ACCEPT NEGATIVITY

A s useful as therapists are, however, they are psychological mercenaries. They can thus supplement or even multiply the value of friendships, but they cannot replace them. Your therapist is a learned and attentive companion, but a friend is a friend for free.

That bond of freely given love and companionship cannot be substituted by even the best therapists in the world, despite how useful therapists may be.

For this reason, one of the best habits you can have, both while you're grieving and while you're not, is the cultivation of friendship.

To cultivate the relationships you want, take a moment to consider energy. Have you ever walked into a room only to be instantly hit with a particular vibe? You may think that it's just your imagination, but it's actually your mind picking up on a wide array of subtle cues that then leave an impression. Consider the energy that you like, and consider the kinds of energy that make you uncomfortable.

Take a moment to consider what kind of energy you wish to attract into your life. Now, take a moment to consider what kind of energy you're giving off. Journaling in the third person may help with this if you haven't tried it already. Now, I've heard people say that opposites attract, but that's only for magnets. You and I, we are not magnets; we are human beings.

Like it or not, the energy you give off is the energy you're going to receive right back. Behave in an abrasive manner, even unintentionally, and people will behave abrasively towards you. Put yourself down all the time, and people will begin to put you down too (unless they're keeping track of all the good you do in the world). Sometimes, a handful of nasty people will treat us badly without provocation, but when we give in and use that as an excuse to behave in negative or self-defeating manners, then we will be treated badly consistently by all but the most compassionate of beings.

This is important to note because energy is recursive; the top five people you keep closest in your life will eventually become the top five people you are most similar to. If you surround yourself with positive people, spend time with them, get to know them, discuss their values, then you too will become more of a positive person. However, "positive" is a bit of a vague term on its own, isn't it?

DEFINING YOUR POSITIVITY

Take a moment to write down the names of your top five friends. These friends can include your partner or spouse, or even people from your family. If you don't feel as if you have many friends, just pick the top five people to whom you relate the most.

Now that you have five names down, take time to write down their good qualities; the things you like, appreciate, or even admire in them. Are they funny? Compassionate? Forgiving? Content? Sensible? Exciting?

Think of how they share these qualities with you. Do these qualities make you feel supported or cared for? Do they make you feel that you're growing, or getting closer to what matters to you in life? Do they make you feel like someone worthy of love? Do you feel secure in your relationship with them? Do you tend to feel content or exhilarated after spending time with them?

If you could answer "yes" to even a few of these, then you're likely already surrounded by the kind of people you need in your life, and you can define your own positivity through examining how they behave.

If you answered "no" to too many of those questions, however, then you may need to consider that you have not yet met everyone who is going to make an impact on your life. If you discover that a relationship has been toxic for you, do not become angry with your friend or lover. Do not actively shun them or cast them out.

We are all different from one another. What makes us happy, what supports us, and what drives us won't always be the same. If a person doesn't make you feel worthy of love, secure or content, that doesn't necessarily mean they're a bad person. Usually, it just means that there's a disconnect in communication that needs to be resolved, and it's fully possible to work your way towards resolving such issues and turning a potentially toxic relationship into a happy and fulfilling one, even if a little counseling is needed.

There's no inherent need to cast out the people who are already around you, but if you find that there are gaps in your emotional needs that need filling, do not be afraid to go out and meet more people, or even switch up the way you spend time with people. Do not be afraid to reach out to people you already know in case of hidden depths, either.

When choosing to develop an existing relationship or start a new one, the best thing you can be is forgiving. Holding onto past faults only breeds resentment, which can turn even the sweetest of bonds into a bitter sauce of strife. Creating resentment can also blind you to your own faults, or cause you to act out against your faults aggressively or destructively, which only causes stunted growth and prolonged grief. When you practice forgiving those around you, don't forget to also practice forgiving yourself. This isn't an excuse for you to do bad things, but rather the acceptance that no one on this Earth is perfect and that, as long as we're alive, we have the opportunity to do better.

To do better, strive to be the kind of person you'd want to meet. This is important as people are attracted to those who are similar to them, but with some unique flair. This unique flair is already part of you; no one else has experienced the exact same combination of successes, failures, development arcs, and perspectives as you.

Focus on developing the parts of you that you wish to see in other people, then you will naturally attract other people with those qualities. You might even surprise yourself by bringing out these qualities in someone you already know. However, you cannot bring out a quality that isn't already there under the surface somewhere, so don't aim to change people; rather, aim to discover what they're willing to share with you.

When you make an effort to discover the qualities you value in those around you, whether they're present in your closest family or briefest acquaintances, you'll naturally feel more in love with life. You may even find yourself naturally letting go of minor anxieties and finding joy even in small things. Not everyone who has these good qualities in your life needs to become someone super-close to you, but by making time to interact with them, you'll naturally create a network that supports you, the way a current of wind effortlessly supports a feather mid-air.

WHY WE NEED POSITIVE PEOPLE IN OUR LIVES

As stated before, we tend to become a mixture of the five people we spend the most time interacting with. This means that by making time for positive individuals we help to erode the negative inner voices we may have.

When one's negative thoughts hold a majority in one's mind, we dehydrate ourselves on a psychological level. Remember those thought-spirals we discussed in Chapter 4? When your thinking is negative, you'll be more naturally inclined to spiral negatively.

This can transform a minor annoyance into a seemingly insurmountable problem. This is what leads us to make mountains out of mole-hills, or to turn a slightly stressful situation into an inescapable nightmare. This negativity, in turn, can cause us to react more aggressively to minor issues, like yelling at a loved one for being unable to teleport. Even though we know they can't bend space and time and appear before us the instant we ask, negative stress-spirals can make us impatient, potentially even beyond reason. This kind of behavior can make it difficult for those you love to grow close to you, as they'll constantly be wondering what little thing will set you off. Meanwhile, you won't be happy either, because your life will feel like an endless stream of one impossible problem after another. The fact that you manage to resolve most of these "impossible" problems will rarely occur to you, because you'll feel so overwhelmed.

Having a supportive group of friends, then, can encourage you to spiral positively instead, or at least prevent you from spiraling too deep into the negative.

This, in turn, can encourage you to think more optimistically. While it's true that excessive optimism can cause a person to waltz into situations woefully underprepared, excessive pessimism is just as bad. When pessimistic inner voices hold a majority in your head, you begin to develop a pessimistic worldview. While the overly-optimistic individual might walk into a scenario underprepared, an overly-pessimistic individual will not walk into a scenario at all, even when they have more than enough to succeed.

Overly-pessimistic people are less likely to recognize their strengths, as well as less likely to recognize when that strength can be used to gain advantages or pursue opportunities. Ironically, this behavior causes the pessimist to fail where they otherwise would have triumphed, reinforcing their negative worldview while keeping them away from their full potential.

A group of supportive friends, therefore, can help motivate you to be the best person you can be, and act as centers of calm in times of stress.

They can help you recognize the positive qualities that you have, even when you weren't aware of them. The best friends tend to pick you up when they know you're down, be playful when they know you're up, and give clear advice when they know you're confused. They won't do this perfectly, of course, but more often or not that's how it will feel when a friend's qualities match up with what you value.

HAPPINESS IS NOT INHERENTLY POSITIVE

At this point, it is important to make a distinction with happiness and positivity, since most of us tend to use the two words interchangeably. Happiness is merely an emotion. Not only that, but it's also a rather fleeting one. Happiness is an intense form of contentment, in the same way that grief is an intense form of sadness. You therefore won't have happiness all the time, and trying to force happiness will only cause existing negative thoughts to entrench themselves more deeply in your psyche.

Positivity is not about what emotions you feel; it is still fully possible for a positive person to cry, or to shout or to sulk, even if they're less likely to do these things than negative people. A positive person is defined not by how they feel, but rather by how they choose to deal with the way they feel, and how they choose to share that feeling with others.

Therefore, the five people you choose to keep closest to you do not have to be the ones who smile or laugh the most. Likewise, you do not need to stress about being happy all the time to achieve positivity. A person who is truly feeling confident in any given moment does not think about questioning whether or not he or she is confident. A person who is upset does not wonder whether or not they are feeling upset. A person who is happy isn't stressing, worrying, or wondering about whether or not they're happy. A happy person simply *is*.

Extending from this, a person seeking happiness will have a great deal of trouble finding it. Happiness can be discerned, but cannot be manufactured. This is because happiness isn't a thing, nor does it live in things. It's simply an emotional response we have depending on other factors going on in our lives. And then, like any other emotion, we'll feel it briefly before we go back to normal.

Building on this, things we enjoy don't necessarily bring happiness. You can enjoy sex, but if you value romance, you won't feel happy unless your romantic life as a whole is in order. You can enjoy food, but you won't feel happy if you aren't sure when you'll next be able to eat, nor will you feel great if your joy is being accompanied by a sense of guilt.

Buying a new car may lead to an enjoyable driving experience, binging alcohol might give you an enjoyable buzz, but in both cases you'll still have to face the next day knowing you blew money on something you didn't need and that doesn't support your values. And then you will not feel happy.

And then, completing the triangle, the things we enjoy aren't what determine our positivity. However, being positive makes you more likely to experience happiness in what you enjoy. Being positive also makes you feel less dependent on happiness, as some of the most common compulsions for seeking happiness–less stress, more satisfaction with life–are already fulfilled by a positive mindset. And what makes a positive mindset isn't what you own; it lies in your ability to connect with others, your ability to process experiences so that you learn even from failures. Positivity is a habit of striving to be empathic and self-aware, and of striving to turn anything that bothers you in life into an opportunity to reflect on what truly matters to you.

So, we cannot gain positivity by relying on things, and we do not depend on happiness for positivity either. Positivity is something we can form in ourselves at any time, although having people around us who support this way of thinking always makes things easier. However, what happens if I am experiencing a negative emotion? How do I deal with that feeling in a positive way?

Even the people we love, the people we draw our positive energy from, will upset us from time to time. In some cases, such as loss, their absence will cause us no end of grief. Forgiveness, as mentioned earlier, is one of the best tools for dealing with negative emotions in a positive manner. But what if we do not feel ready to forgive?

Firstly, recognize that being positive doesn't mean you need to feel positive 100% of the time. Once again, it's not about what you feel, it's about how you choose to deal with it. Not how you dealt with it in the past, or how you will deal with it in the future; how you are dealing with it now, in this very moment. No one is perfect, and believing you aren't allowed to falter in order to be defined as positive will only put you in a negative mindset.

When you're dealing with negative emotions, it's wise to instead perform a value-check on yourself. Ask yourself, "What is important to me in life? How do I spend my time? What do I make time for in my life?" and then, finally, "Do these actions align with what I believe to be right?"

Consider what you believe to be right, and then do your best to express your negative emotion in the context of that value. There is nothing wrong with experiencing negativity. However, negative feelings or experiences can pull us down if we act on them without keeping our values in mind, whether we value peace, family, love, honor, or integrity. When dealing with a bad feeling while keeping what matters to us in mind, however, it can transform into a building block for us to construct a stronger life on.

9

ESCAPE THE VICTIM MENTALITY

W hile it is true that our friends can help us feel more positive, it does not then follow that they're responsible for our positivity. As the saying goes, you can lead a horse to water, but you cannot make it drink.

A good selection of friends can encourage and support your efforts to grow as a person and find greater joy in all aspects of life, but ultimately you are the one responsible for constructing and maintaining that mindset. You are the architect of your soul.

In wealthy societies, and for many individuals raised in a consumerist culture, one's life is so full of things that it's difficult to decide what to care about anymore. This can, in turn, make it harder to determine our values which, in turn, can make dealing with difficult experiences in a positive manner much trickier than they otherwise would be.

Complicating matters further is how positivity is marketed towards us. As nice as it is, it is unhealthy to try to pursue positivity all the time.

It is healthy to know what you want, and it is good to establish relations with those who are supportive of you. However, you must be careful not to let your goals devolve into a vague or abstract desire for "positivity." When we do that, we tend to then fall into the trap of obsessively pursuing joy or happiness.

Now, there's nothing wrong with experiencing joy or happiness; they're both wonderful things to feel. However, remember what was said earlier; the happy person isn't trying to be happy. They simply are. Happiness, joy and even positivity are all like wild animals that you're trying to soothe and tame.

You won't catch it if you try to chase it; in fact, in chasing it you're more likely to kill it than tame it. The best you can do, then, is encourage it to come to you. This is why Chapter 8 encourages you to invite positivity into your life by being aware of what you want and making time to interact with people who have similar interests. Friendship with those who genuinely value and care about you is a wonderful thing and an amazing way to entice positivity into our lives! But what if we try to chase positivity directly?

When we cultivate a powerful desire to chase positivity, we only make ourselves more aware of the negativity in our lives. In extreme cases, it can even blind you to the good that you already have. Think of any of the more obsessive corporate climbers you may know, who pursue wealth only to never feel quite rich enough despite earning a

6-figure salary and potentially possessing thousands, or even millions of dollars in assets.

Likewise, think of the individual who pursues someone without taking to account what we discussed in Chapter 8. They'll work hard to make themselves attractive, and yet in the end they'll only make themselves feel ugly and unwanted because they keep trying to interface with someone who doesn't hold the same values. They'll feel unwanted, even when they're adored by people around them, because when one focuses on the pursuit one tends to tune out what's sitting in one's peripheral vision.

In the same way that obsessively chasing wealth or attractiveness will leave you feeling the opposite, so too will obsessively chasing positivity leave you feeling negative in the long run. In all these cases, you're desiring to fill a perceived emptiness in your life, whether it exists or not. The longer you chase, the worse and more real this emptiness becomes.

So think of positivity not as a matter of desire or pursuit, but rather as a matter of appreciation. When you let yourself experience appreciation for what's around you, and when you allow that appreciation to enter your core as a human being, you'll naturally invite positivity into your life in a healthy and long-lasting manner. Cherish the good things that already exist in your life, and positivity will naturally manifest itself around you without you having to chase it. This is because instead of trying to fill a perceived emptiness with external things, you're instead taking stock of the fullness that already exists in your life.

But what about the negativity that exists in one's life? Although counter-intuitive, accepting negativity can lead to greater positivity in the long run, just like how focusing too much on chasing "positive" things could make us feel worse.

But what does it mean to accept negativity? Accepting negativity does not mean being pessimistic. Rather, it means realizing that bad things will happen occasionally and that, while one must do what they can about it according to their true values (remember that rest, comfort and self-care are values too), it's not worth getting ensnared by it.

To accept negativity, then, does not mean letting oneself be surrounded by it. Rather, accepting negativity means being conscious of its existence, and then being okay with letting it go, similarly to how you'd let go of a bad thought spiral during meditation. Letting go doesn't mean denial; it means acknowledgment, followed by the assertion that your current thoughts and feelings do not have to define your entire reality. Thoughts and feelings can change easily from one moment to the next, and yet reality carries on around us as it always does.

ESTABLISHING AGENCY

So, why was all of the above relevant in terms of escaping the victim mentality? What's hopefully clear by now is that reality is what it is, no matter how we choose to think or feel about it. That said, we *do* have the power to change the way we interact with that reality. We also have the power to change which part of that reality we're most often surrounded by. Furthermore, it is our own behavior that determines whether we remain a victim or become an active living body once again. And, finally, just because we have been behaving like a victim for the past few days, months or years doesn't mean it's too late to start looking at the world differently.

Now, this is not to say that everything bad that happens to you is your fault; it's not. I know for my grief, it was not my choice to lose my mother. I was powerless to stop that. However, I began to feel powerless all the time. Every time something bad happened, such as a teacher snapping at a student and giving them detention for a minor accident, being turned down for multiple job interviews despite having good grades and hearty letters of recommendation, people making unwelcome comments on my appearance... I just accepted these things, thinking the world was an awful place and that nothing could be done to change it.

Although the world can be awful, my budding victim mentality fooled me into thinking all of it was awful, all the time.

A victim mentality is one of the most disempowering things you can have. It is a form of deep pessimism that encourages you to believe that just because you cannot control some of the things in your life, you are therefore unable to control anything in your life. This is a logical fallacy. I might not be able to control whether it is raining or not, but I can control whether or not I bring an umbrella or thermal jacket when I step outside. I might not be able to control when I feel happy or joyful, but I can control whether I surround myself with people that I value, or participate in events that line up with my principles.

Likewise, thinking back, I could've spoken to the teacher and shown them compassion by asking how their day has been. If I had a major problem with the punishment of the student, I could've talked to the student council or even the principal. And if they wouldn't listen, I could've talked to the student and their parents and offered sympathy, and if the issue was worth kicking a fuss up about, I could've helped them do that too. There's always some way for us to change our circumstances, and even the smallest steps are better than taking none at all. When I was grieving, I wanted help, sympathy and support, but I was blind to the fact that everyone around me needed these things too. As much as I was willing to get, I needed to also be willing to give before I could experience true healing.

Eventually, I found a job by remaining persistent and keeping an open mind in case an unexpected opportunity came up, and being heckled on the street didn't matter once I realized that the opinions of strangers have no inherent power over me and I don't have to care what they think.

We are not perpetual victims. Although we may be tricked, hit, bamboozled, and hurt, the victimhood incurred by such actions is temporary. While it is important to let yourself feel the emotions associated with being betrayed or attacked, endeavor to never use these feelings as an excuse to stop striving for the kind of life you want, or the values you believe in.

What you want or value can change over time, of course; the more we learn, the more our conscious values change as we grow closer to our true selves, so there's no shame in conceding a belief. The point is that when we make the choice to change, it should always be for the sake of growth and life, not for the sake of shrinking into our own shadows.

When examining the functionally positive and successful people around you, you might notice that when something bad happens in their lives, they will take some measure of responsibility for it. A newly promoted manager who goes, "Argh, I'm being swamped by so much work all of a sudden! The corporation doesn't care about me, treating me like some dumb cog in their dumb machine. This job sucks!" isn't going to be a manager for long, or at least not a very good one. The kind of attitude shown above tends to lead to laziness, cantankerous behavior and a scared or demotivated workforce.

In contrast, imagine a newly promoted manager saying, "Wow, this is a hell of a lot of work compared to what I'm used to, but I guess that's what it takes to do this job. Well, they wouldn't have promoted me if they didn't think I was ready, so I'll give it a try and do the best I can."

Unlike the first manager, this manager isn't boxing themselves into the victim mentality. Out of the two managers, which one do you think sounds most likely to approach a colleague if they need help? The one who wants to do the best they can, or the one who believes that they're seen as just a lonely cog in an unfeeling machine? Out of the two managers, which one do you think is more likely to speak honestly (read: without shifting blame or hiding the issue behind flattery or excuses) and seek support from their supervisors if things aren't going well? The one who assumes their supervisors don't care and are out to get them, or the one who believes their supervisors want to see them succeed?

Out of the two managers, which one is more likely to get the help they need and achieve success? The one who chooses to communicate with their superiors and interface with their colleagues, of course! Trust me when I tell you that a person who compares themselves to a powerless cog in their own narratives and assumes everyone is against them *isn't* going to be the one who'll effectively gain this help, even if they need it.

YOU HAVE POWER OVER YOUR FATE

Even if the 2 managers above were equal in all other aspects, that difference in attitude is what would've made the difference between success and failure. In both cases, they can't control that they've just been given a large workload, but they can control how they perceive the issue at hand, which in turn can subtly influence how they go about resolving it.

Even if the task truly is insurmountable, the manager who has avoided victim mentality won't take failure or even demotion personally; they'll simply return to what they know they're good at and keep practicing it until another opportunity for growth presents itself. The manager who has avoided victim mentality is also less likely to lash out or become embittered with those around them, meaning even though things didn't go so well, they at least haven't completely shut the door on trying again.

When you accept that you can take charge of your life, even if it's just some aspects of it, you not only become more powerful in your personal affairs, you become more charismatic, as giving yourself direction makes it easier for you to direct others when they are unsure or confused.

When you are stuck with the victim mentality, however, you depend on people completely and utterly to do things for you. This is fine for short periods, but people will struggle to help you for long when you're this dependent, as most won't know what you truly want. And when they don't know what you want, they're far more likely to return to sorting out their own lives than guess at how to resolve yours. Usually, only parents have the patience to guess what the problem is in cases like this, and even then only when dealing with infants or small children who can't be expected to communicate effectively yet.

In contrast, when you're able to acknowledge responsibility for your life, people find it much easier to assist you when you feel stuck because you're at least acting as the driving force in your own narrative, rather than forcing them to do it.

When you maintain the drive to guide or lead sympathetic efforts in your own life as you resolve personal issues, people feel more secure that what they're doing for you matters, and that you'd be able to help them in turn if they needed it. They render their aid to you feeling warm and satisfied, and a feeling of appreciation forms between you both, contributing to healthy positivity.

On the other hand, when we consistently sit around and list off all our own aches, pains and grievances without exploring ways to solve them on our own time, we end up becoming psychological vampires who drain anyone who comes near us of their time and energy, leaving them feeling tired and empty rather than satisfied. We also end up becoming more entitled if such a victim mentality persists long enough on our part, since we grow more and more accustomed to people simply swooping in and magically fixing all our problems without us having to do anything more than complain.

That said, if you are currently suffering from victim mentality, do not stress. By taking control of small things in your life, but realizing that not everything needs to be interfered with, and you'll come closer to breaking free of your victim mentality.

By being aware of your emotional wants and needs, but recognizing it is better to invite than to chase, you break free of your victim mentality. By being forgiving, you break free; blaming people less means you assign responsibility to others less, meaning you are less likely to construct self-destructive narratives where they hold all the power and you have no say. You become less likely to trap yourself mentally. Writing, reading, exercising and meditating all encourage you to empower yourself, take some action in your life—even if it's small—and thus break free of perpetual victimhood.

Those who suffer from grief are victims, but not forever. By avoiding the cultivation of a perpetual victim mentality, you reduce your chances of worsening into complicated grief, and from there remain in a better position to address what truly matters to you in the way that *you* want to address it. Victim mentality forces us to grieve on everyone else's timetable, but proper healing through grief requires us to take time for ourselves.

10

ACCEPT RESPONSIBILITY FOR YOURSELF

To ensure you stay free of perpetual victim-mentality, however, you need to take more and more responsibility for your own wellbeing–whether that is physical, emotional or intellectual.

Remember when we spoke about how amazingly awesome positive friends can be? We also touched on how it is nevertheless poor form to hold them responsible for our positivity. In the end, working towards your positivity requires a series of choices that must be made personally by you.

However, I don't think we've fully explored what the consequences can be when we do place the responsibility for our wellbeing in the hands of others.

ACCEPT RESPONSIBILITY FOR YOUR EMOTIONS

When we believe a person, most commonly a lover or spouse, is responsible for the way we feel, we tend to blame them for *our* negative emotions. Yet, when we blame someone else for what we feel, strange things start to happen.

Firstly, when we make a person responsible for the way we feel, we also imply that we are responsible for the way they feel too. This is because one-sided responsibility strongly resembles a parent-child relationship. This isn't a functional way for adults to relate to one another, so most people who want the relationship to continue when they're blamed for their partner's emotions will start blaming their partner in turn. This leads to, and reinforces, emotional codependency between the two partners.

However, this mutual codependence doesn't make things better. When we hold each other responsible for how we feel, rather than ourselves, we both become more likely to enter the victim mentality together. Personal boundaries fly out the window, but in a way that is scary and constrictive rather than sexy or intimate.

This leads to a situation where neither partner feels safe doing *anything* without the approval of the other. Whether it's deciding on dinner, deciding what to watch on TV or even deciding how to spend alone time when apart, everything eventually ends up being cross-checked. Our lives eventually revolve around the emotional wellbeing of the other.

Now, it is natural to care for one another in any form of relationship, whether romantic or platonic. This is normal and healthy. However, when this care is not only taken for granted, but *expected* to be prioritized 24/7, then there will invariably be great resentments. When we start getting mad at someone close to us because they fail to be fully devoted to us 24/7, then not only are we making the mistake of assuming them to be perfect or divine (and also making the mistake of assuming that what's perfect for us is perfect for everyone), we're also being extraordinarily selfish by refusing to consider what is going on in *their* lives that might be distracting or upsetting them.

Likewise, we can become bitter towards someone if they treat us this way too, and this bitterness not only leads to otherwise avoidable conflicts and grief, it can also encourage us to form bad habits (such as manipulation) as we resort to do anything to satisfy our partner's feelings or desires, even if that "satisfaction" is brought about by a combination of guilt, shame and trickery.

When we create an environment where love or support is given out of *obligation* or *expectation* rather than *choice*, we also create an environment that encourages us to hide how we truly feel and manipulate what we think our partner feels.

When we accept responsibility for our own feelings, however, and trust our partner to do the same, we make room in our lives for freely-given love. Freely-given love between two people creates an environment where we don't automatically assume the worst of our partner just because they aren't being especially supportive on a given day. Instead of weaving a narrative where they're heartless or insensitive, in a situation of freely-given love we are more likely to be honest with our emotions and ask for help if we need it.

ACCEPT RESPONSIBILITY FOR YOUR OWN STANDARDS

Remember, accepting responsibility for yourself is the antithesis of being trapped in a perpetual malaise of victimhood. Part of this involves accepting responsibility for your standards: the metrics by which you judge others or judge yourself.

It's always important to criticize our metrics, as the ways we choose to measure ourselves aren't always realistic. You can be a smart, funny and good-looking individual, yet still feel stupid, boring or ugly because of a self-limiting value metric.

For instance, maybe you grew up to be much shorter than you expected. Maybe, because you're shorter than most people you know, you feel ugly and that no one will ever love you. This is an example of an extremely limiting belief; when we define our worth based on a system of measurement we have no control over, we disempower ourselves. It's not your fault that you're short. It's not something you chose. So, why define your self-worth based on your height? Out of all your other qualities, why *height?* Would you judge others based solely on the distance between their head and the ceiling? Probably not, because most of us realize how superficial such a measurement system is when applied to others. So why are we applying it to ourselves?

Maybe you aren't as muscular as you would like to be. This is something you have some choice over, but despite valuing muscles maybe you don't value the processes behind muscle-building enough to follow through, causing an inner conflict. To help resolve this conflict, think of the best people in your life. Is it their muscles that made them such wonderful people? Even for athletes, the appearance of their muscles isn't as important as what those muscles let them do on the field, and only then because it's important to their passion and career. If you judged all your friends primarily by their muscles, you'd certainly miss out on a treasure trove of their deeper qualities. Likewise, judging yourself by such a metric could make you miss out on yours.

When you find that your standards are bringing you down or making you feel inferior, it is best to perform a value-check on yourself. In the case of our hypothetical height scenario, why do you value the idea of being tall? Usually, one values the idea of being tall because we feel it makes us attractive. However, being tall isn't the only way to be attractive. In that case, someone who felt ugly because they're short could overcome their limiting belief by exploring other ways of being attractive; being clever, witty, or interesting. Overcoming a limiting belief also makes you inherently more attractive, since it helps you feel more secure in yourself and avoid being the psychological vampire we mentioned earlier. On the physical side, there's also nothing stopping you from keeping yourself well-groomed or pulling off a rugged charm; these qualities are independent of height.

In the muscle scenario, why do you value the idea of being strong? The 3 biggest reasons tend to be, "I want to look more attractive", "I want to be healthier", and "I want to get better at protecting those I care about". Not everyone builds muscles as easily; bodybuilders in particular MUST live by a very strict diet that is neither practical nor enjoyable for most people. In the case of attractiveness, see the previous paragraph. In the case of being healthier, why are muscles important for that? If you aren't getting sick that often, and are fit enough to accomplish the work of your average day while remaining in a good mood, then you're healthy, regardless of your muscle mass.

In the case of protection, your mind is much more important than your muscles; tactics, technique, quick-thinking, perception, preparation will all help you protect yourself without you needing great strength at all. Don't get caught up in surface goals like, "I want to be richer, stronger, more beautiful, more powerful." Always ask yourself WHY you want these things, and then think of alternate ways to satisfy that root motivation. If you can't think of alternate ways, borrow a book on subjects similar to your root motive. There are always options for achieving a root goal.

This also goes for when the root goal is something like becoming smarter, discovering something new, finding inner peace or cultivating love; the large number of viable religious, philosophical and political belief systems show this quite handily, as if the wide and diverse fields of knowledge available in the world didn't demonstrate that on its own.

When we question the root cause of our standards and values, we're able to change and improve them for the better. It also makes it easier for us to play to our strengths, since considering the reasoning behind our standards makes it easier for us to find alternative ways to achieve the aim that our standards were intended to encourage.

The values and metrics by which you measure yourself are entirely your choices. While you can blame others for encouraging you to think or measure yourself a certain way, in the end you are the one responsible for changing how you think if you don't believe it's working. No matter what people have done or how they behaved in the past, you are responsible for what you choose to do next in life.

ACCEPT RESPONSIBILITY FOR YOUR PROBLEMS

It wasn't my fault that I had to deal with grief over my mother, but it was still my responsibility to deal with it. I am responsible for the choices I made. I am responsible for how I felt.

It wasn't my dad's fault that he had to deal with grief over my mother either, but it was still his responsibility to continue being a parent and raise me. Now, technically, all he had to do was keep me alive and attending school. In his grief, he could've chosen to do not an ounce more than that. However, responsibility doesn't just apply to what we're expected to do, it applies to anything we have some measure of power or control over, and while people might not blame us beyond our obligations, all of our responsibilities carry wider consequences. If my dad couldn't accept his wider, unobligated responsibilities and got stuck in a victim mentality, school would've been a lot harder for me. We might've even lost the house, and an already difficult situation would have spiraled into something much worse as a result. But, because he continued being responsible for everything he could still realistically control, my dad made sure that although some parts of life sucked, there'd still be some spaces that were safe and comfortable. He made sure I always had a cozy place to do my homework, and that I always had access to any books or stationery I needed. He also did his best to comfort me, although I didn't always listen. He couldn't control whether or not I sincerely took what he said to heart, but he could control whether or not he'd present the foundations for an epiphany to me. He didn't let my obstinate nature (I was a teen at the time, to be fair) push him into a victim mentality. He just kept focusing on what he could do, and through that brought about positive change.

Going further, it wasn't the doctor's fault that my mother died. Maybe, in his mind, he could've done a better job trying to save her, but from my point of view he'd done everything he could. When terminal illness was confirmed, he could've chosen to act like a victim and believe that, because he couldn't save her, he couldn't do anything else further. Luckily, that's not the choice he made. He recognized that, while he was no longer practically responsible for her life, he was still responsible for her comfort. He couldn't realistically control whether she lived or died, but he could at least make sure she died as painlessly as possible, and that he'd keep giving her the best fighting chance he could until that happened. He could also control whether or not he'd try to comfort us after she passed away. Thanks to his actions, what would otherwise have been a wholly traumatic event at least carried the solace that the people looking after our mother in hospital *cared* for her. It was remembering this act of care that eventually helped me pull myself out of my own state of victim mentality, as it directly challenged my misguided worldview that I lived in a cold and heartless society.

And, of course, it wasn't my mother's fault that she was so ill. This won't be true for everyone that is dying, but whether it's the person's fault or not doesn't matter at that stage; when something is someone's fault, it meant they made a mistake in the past. Responsibility is how we choose to deal with things in the present, regardless of whether they're our fault or not.

For my mother, her responsibility was making the best of her remaining time on this Earth. She seemed to slow down a bit, as if she was now taking the time to truly pay attention to everything, and she managed to smile and laugh a lot more because of this, even though we could all see she was in great pain. She continued enjoying life with us as much as she could, until she was bedridden in the hospital and it became our responsibility to be there for her. Again, responsibility is not the same as obligation; we could've chosen to just leave her there and begin grieving immediately. We weren't legally or even socially obligated by anyone to go see her during her stay in the hospital once she was admitted. But we valued her, and although we couldn't control whether or not she lived another day, we could control whether or not we pitched up and made ourselves part of those last days.

Because we chose to act on what we could control, we could at least say goodbye, and had plenty of opportunities to share corny jokes and anecdotes from her life I'd otherwise never known.

Because she chose to act on what she could control, she helped lay a positive foundation. All these years after the worst of my grief has long departed, I still remember how brave and spirited she was. I still remember the love in her eyes, and I remember how weakly her hand would grab onto mine in her last few days. Her choice to act on what she could control meant that even after she had passed on, there was never a moment of doubt - in my dad's, brother's or my heart- that she loved us dearly, and that she knew we loved her.

Imagine if she'd instead embraced her potential victim mentality; if she used her impending death as an excuse to do nothing, say nothing and just sequester herself away to perish. We'd never have found any closure, and life may have turned out very differently for my dad, brother, and I.

So, as much as possible, take responsibility for the problems that come up in your life. Taking responsibility doesn't mean solving them single-handedly, but it does mean standing up in defiance against the idea that you're powerless. It means acting in whatever small way you can to make life better along the threads that you control. It means accepting that even the smallest positive differences are worth making. Every brush stroke in a painting makes up the artwork. Every layer of paint contributes to the final piece.

So take responsibility for your life as much as you can. Every positive brushstroke you make will help build up the artwork that is your life, so that you can look at it with satisfaction, and that those you love can look at it and find peace.

CONCLUSION

Although this is the end of this book, this is not the end of your journey. Everyone grieves differently, there's no need to rush your healing. However, continue to practice what you've learned as best you can. If you need more answers, do not hesitate to read further from a wide variety of authors; every writer's differing perspective of a topic will help you build a more universal view.

To solidify that view and order the chaotic thoughts one often experiences during grief, remember to ink down the breathings of your heart. No matter how you feel about something, spending a few minutes writing about it can help you spot patterns you may have otherwise missed. And, when the subject matter becomes too heavy or overwhelming even to write through, take a breather by sitting down and letting yourself meditate for a few minutes.

Do the best you can to look after yourself physically; make proper time for sleep so that your body and mind both get the rest they need to function properly. Drink liquids, eat food, and move your body so that you begin to feel better each day. Let the oxygen in your blood flow freely through your veins. Scrape the rust off your joints with stretches so that you don't have to fight your body as well as your grief.

As much as you can, be honest about how you feel, both in your writing and in your speech. In times of trouble, keep your five favorite people as close to you as you can, and don't be afraid to hire professional assistance to fill in the gaps.

But most of all, remember that how you deal with grief is on you. The people around you can support and help you, but in the end the decision to heal is down to you. This means you can take as long as you need to heal, regardless of what others say. But it also means you're responsible for the consequences of what you do; if something goes wrong, you're the most reliable person to fix it. If you don't know how to fix it, you're the most reliable person to find someone who can.

The important thing is that you never forget you're allowed to take charge of your life, and you're especially allowed to take charge of how you deal with your grief. The advice in this book simply consists of some of the healthier ways that I found worked for me, based on more than a decade of almost getting it right and then messing up spectacularly.

I compiled all I have learned in the hope that you won't mess up as much, but even if you do, the next important thing is that you never give up. The moment you give up is the moment you stop taking charge of your own healing. The moment you get back up again is the moment you come closer to achieving the life you want.

Don't waste energy chasing after things that can be gained through self-reflection. Don't disempower yourself by blaming others for how you feel and, if you ever do blame someone else, dare to make amends as best you can, both for your sake and for theirs. However, don't blame yourself either. Not everything bad in life has to be assigned as someone's fault. This grief isn't your fault, it isn't anyone's fault. But it is your responsibility. It's like a baby on your doorstep; it may not have come about by your actions, but its fate is now in your hands. So, most of all, be gentle with it.

If you have found this book helpful, please consider helping others by leaving a review on Amazon. I'll be happy to read it and learn from your perspective, much as I hope you've learned from mine. Others who are looking for answers will also use your review to help guide them to where they need to be, so it truly would be appreciated.

It's been my pleasure to share this knowledge with you. Now, go forth and use it to help your world shine light through the rains of grief.

REFERENCES

Ackerman, C. (2020, February 11). *Trauma-Focused Cognitive Behavioral Therapy: Life After Freud.* PositivePsychology.Com.

https://positivepsychology.com/trauma-focused-cognitive-behavioral-therapy/

Aqtai, A. (2019). Brown Desk Lamp on Table. In *Pexels.*

https://www.pexels.com/photo/brown-desk-lamp-on-table-2233416/

Ardagh, P. (2008). *Philip Ardagh's Book of Absolutely Useless Lists for Absolutely Every Day of the Year.* Macmillan.

ArtHouse Studio. (2020). Relaxed Woman in White Bathrobe Reading Ebook. In *Pexels.* https://www.pexels.com/photo/relaxed-woman-in-white-bathrobe-reading-ebook-4353680/

Baikie, K., & Wilhelm, K. (2005). Emotional and Physical Health Benefits of Expressive Writing. *Advances in Psychiatric Treatment*, 11(5), 338–346.

https://doi.org/10.1192/apt.11.5.338

Bernardo, C. (2016, January 5). *Grief and Nutrition: Tips From a Wellness Guru*. What's Your Grief.

https://whatsyourgrief.com/grief-and-nutrition/

Bertelli, M. (2017). Woman Using Umbrella With Lights. In *Pexels*.

https://www.pexels.com/photo/astronomy-dark-dawn-dusk-573238/

Brown, L. F., Reynolds, C. F., Monk, T. H., Prigerson, H. G., Dew, M. A., Houck, P. R., Mazumdar, S., Buysse, D. J., Hoch, C. C., & Kupfer, D. J. (1996). Social Rhythm Stability Following Late-Life Spousal Bereavement: Associations With Depression and Sleep Impairment. *Psychiatry Research*, 62(2), 161–169.

https://doi.org/10.1016/0165-1781(96)02914-9

Buxbaum, J. (2016, April 1). *8 Unexpected Ways Books Can Help You Through Grief*. Bustle.

https://www.bustle.com/articles/151288-8-unexpected-ways-books-can-help-you-through-grief-and-loss

Cherney, K. (2018, November 66). *How Long Does Caffeine Stay in Your System?* Healthline; Healthline Media.

https://www.healthline.com/health/how-long-does-caffeine-last

Colier, N. (2018, January 12). *Are You Ready to Stop Feeling Like a Victim?* Psychology Today. https://www.psychologytoday.com/ca/blog/inviting-monkey-tea/201801/are-you-ready-stop-feeling-victim

Constance, K. (2019). Woman Sitting on Wooden Planks. In *Pexels*.

https://www.pexels.com/photo/woman-sitting-on-wooden-planks-2865901/

Cottonbro. (2020a). Sticky Notes on Glass Wall. In *Pexels*.

https://www.pexels.com/photo/sticky-notes-on-glass-wall-3831847/

Cottonbro. (2020b). Person in Black Pants and Black Shoes Sitting on Brown Wooden Chair. In *Pexels*.

https://www.pexels.com/photo/person-in-black-pants-and-black-shoes-sitting-on-brown-wooden-chair-4101143/

Cushner, K. (2018, March 12). *How to Fall Back Asleep If You Wake Up.* Tuck Sleep.

https://www.tuck.com/fall-back-asleep/

Denis E. Boyd & Associates Inc. (2020). *Brooke Lewis.* Denis Boyd & Associates Psychologists & Counsellors.

https://www.denisboyd.com/about-us/therapists/brooke-lewis/

DeNoon, D. J. (2008, May 30). *Exercise and Depression.* WebMD.

https://www.webmd.com/depression/guide/exercise-depression#1

Domingues, C. (2017). Closeup Photography of Adult Short-Coated Tan and White Dog Sleeping on Gray Textile at Daytime. In *Pexels*.

https://www.pexels.com/photo/closeup-photography-of-adult-short-coated-tan-and-white-dog-sleeping-on-gray-textile-at-daytime-731022/

Frey, M. (2019, May 27). *Exercise and Nutrition Tips to Ease the Grieving Process*. Verywell Fit.

https://www.verywellfit.com/exercise-and-nutrition-tips-to-ease-the-grieving-process-4160071

Frey, M. (2020, May 29). *8 Easy Workouts for Beginners*. Verywell Fit.

https://www.verywellfit.com/easy-weight-loss-workouts-for-beginners-3495986

Fring, G. (2020a). Man Lying With Journal Sharing Problems With Advisor. In *Pexels*.

https://www.pexels.com/photo/man-lying-with-journal-sharing-problems-with-advisor-4148892/

Fring, G. (2020b). Smiling Students Discussing Day in College. In *Pexels*.

https://www.pexels.com/photo/smiling-students-discussing-day-in-college-4172961/

Goncharenok, M. (2020). Photo of Man Lying on Concrete Floor. In *Pexels*.

https://www.pexels.com/photo/photo-of-man-lying-on-concrete-floor-4663822/

Harvey, S. B., Øverland, S., Hatch, S. L., Wessely, S., Mykletun, A., & Hotopf, M. (2017). Exercise and the Prevention of Depression: Results of the HUNT Cohort Study. *American Journal of Psychiatry*, 175(1), 28–36.

https://doi.org/10.1176/appi.ajp.2017.16111223

Hotchandani, E. (2020). *Home | Eric Hotchandani | Marriage and Family Counseling.* Eric Hotchandani, LMFT.

https://www.erichotchandani.com/

Hugstad, K. (2017, June 19). *What to Eat When Grief Is Eating You.* HuffPost. https://www.huffpost.com/entry/what-to-eat-when-grief-is-eating-you_b_59481460e4b0f7875b83e4ad

Inouye, M. (2019). Self Care Isn't Selfish Signage. In *Pexels.*

https://www.pexels.com/photo/self-care-isn-t-selfish-signage-2821823/

Jewell, T. (2014, January 22). *Depression vs. Complicated Grief.* Healthline; Healthline Media.

https://www.healthline.com/health/depression/complicated-grief#symptoms

Kaboompics.com. (2015). Woman's Hand Using a Pen Noting on Notepad. In *Pexels.* https://www.pexels.com/photo/woman-s-hand-using-a-pen-noting-on-notepad-6360/

Kentish-Barnes, N., Chaize, M., Seegers, V., Legriel, S., Cariou, A., Jaber, S., Lefrant, J.-Y., Floccard, B., Renault, A., Vinatier, I., Mathonnet, A., Reuter, D., Guisset, O., Cohen-Solal, Z., Cracco, C., Seguin, A., Durand-Gasselin, J., Éon, B., Thirion, M., … Azoulay, É. (2015). Complicated Grief After Death of a Relative in the Intensive Care Unit. *European Respiratory Journal*, 45(5), 1341–1352.

https://doi.org/10.1183/09031936.00160014

Kilroy, D. (2019, February 27). *Eating the Right Foods for Exercise.* Healthline; Healthline Media.

https://www.healthline.com/health/fitness-exercise-eating-healthy#carbohydrates

Knott, L. (2017, September 11). Depression. Patient.

https://patient.info/mental-health/depression-leaflet

Kornfield, J. (2017, September 13). *A Meditation on Grief.* Jack Kornfield.

https://jackkornfield.com/meditation-grief/

Kos, B. (2016, March 10). *Why You Should Read Every Day.* Agile-LeanLife.

https://agileleanlife.com/why-you-should-read-every-day/

Lehman, S. (2020, April 1). *An Overview of Nutrition for a Better Diet.* Verywell Fit.

https://www.verywellfit.com/nutrition-basics-4157080

Manson, M. (2020). *Personal Values: A Guide to Figuring Out Who You Are*. Mark Manson.

https://markmanson.net/values/personal-values-guide

Neimeyer, R., Hardison, H., & Lichstein, K. (2005). Insomnia and Complicated Grief Symptoms in Bereaved College Students. *Behavioral Sleep Medicine*, 3(2), 99–111.

https://doi.org/10.1207/s15402010bsm0302_4

Pasternak, R. E., Reynolds, C. F., Hoch, C. C., Buysse, D. S., Schlernitzauer, M., Machen, M., & Kupfer, D. J. (1992). Sleep in Spousally Bereaved Elders With Subsyndromal Depressive Symptoms. *Psychiatry Research*, 43(1), 43–53.

https://doi.org/10.1016/0165-1781(92)90140-x

Piacquadio, A. (2020a). Woman Draw a Light Bulb in White Board. In *Pexels*.

https://www.pexels.com/photo/woman-draw-a-light-bulb-in-white-board-3758105/

Piacquadio, A. (2020b). Photo of Man in Gray T-Shirt and Black Jeans on Sitting on Wooden Floor Meditating. In *Pexels*.

https://www.pexels.com/photo/photo-of-man-in-gray-t-shirt-and-black-jeans-on-sitting-on-wooden-floor-meditating-3760611/

Salla, S. (2019, April 1). *#8 Ways to Surround Yourself With Positive Energy*. Entrepreneur.

https://www.entrepreneur.com/article/331564

Sample, I. (2009, February 15). *Keeping a Diary Makes You Happier*. The Guardian.

https://www.theguardian.com/science/2009/feb/15/psychology-usa

Sayles, B. (2019). Two Men and Woman Sitting Next to Each Other. In *Pexels*.

https://www.pexels.com/photo/two-men-and-woman-sitting-next-to-each-other-2479312/

Scott, E. (2020, February 13). *4 Ways to Surround Yourself With Positive Energy*. Verywell Mind.

https://www.verywellmind.com/reduce-stress-positive-energy-3144815

Singh, Y. (2018). Man Walking Near Body of Water. In *Pexels*.

https://www.pexels.com/photo/man-walking-near-body-of-water-1466852/

Smith, L. (2018, May 16). *Can Exercise Help Those Dealing With Grief?* Patient.

https://patient.info/news-and-features/can-exercise-help-with-grief

Snapwire. (2017). Close-Up Photography of Lighted Candles. In *Pexels*.

https://www.pexels.com/photo/close-up-photography-of-lighted-candles-722653/

Stang, H. (2020, April 19). *Grief Journaling Tips & Writing Prompts for Meaning Making After Loss.* Mindfulness & Grief.

https://mindfulnessandgrief.com/grief-journaling/

Stutzer, A. (2018, March 22). *How Does Your Smartphone Affect Your Sleep?* Tuck Sleep.

https://www.tuck.com/smartphones-and-sleep/

Tartakovsky, M. (2019, June 7). Benefits of Therapy You Probably Didn't Know About. PsychCentral.

https://psychcentral.com/blog/benefits-of-therapy-you-probably-didnt-know-about/

Tentis, D. (2017). Cooked Meat With Vegetables. In *Pexels*.

https://www.pexels.com/photo/cooked-meat-with-vegetables-725991/

The Survival Journal Editorial Staff. (2020). The Survival Rule of Threes. The Survival Journal.

https://thesurvivaljournal.com/survival-rule-of-threes/

Tran, B. (2018). Dont Wish for It Work for It Calligraphy. In *Pexels*.

https://www.pexels.com/photo/dont-wish-for-it-work-for-it-calligraphy-1074920/

Tuck Sleep. (2019a, July 18). *The Best and Worst Foods for a Good Night's Sleep.* Tuck Sleep.

https://www.tuck.com/foods-that-help-you-sleep/

Tuck Sleep. (2019b, July 21). *Sleep Deprivation - Causes, Dangers, Prevention, Treatment*. Tuck Sleep.

https://www.tuck.com/sleep-deprivation/

Tuck Sleep. (2020a, January 9). *Create an Ideal Environment for Sleep*. Tuck Sleep.

https://www.tuck.com/optimize-your-sleep-environment/

Tuck Sleep. (2020b, March 31). *Health Benefits of Napping*. Tuck Sleep.

https://www.tuck.com/napping/

Tuck Sleep. (2020c, April 22). *Women and Insomnia: Menopause, Pregnancy, and PMS*. Tuck Sleep.

https://www.tuck.com/sleep-disorders/insomnia-women/

Tuck Sleep. (2020d, May 5). *Grief and Sleep Issues: How to Sleep Better During Bereavement*. Tuck Sleep.

https://www.tuck.com/sleep-and-grief/

Tuck Sleep. (2020e, May 18). *Ultimate Guide to Melatonin and Sleep*. Tuck Sleep.

https://www.tuck.com/melatonin/

Wong, C. (2020, February 3). *The 20 Best Food Sources of Antioxidants*. Verywell Fit.

https://www.verywellfit.com/best-food-sources-of-antioxidants-88392

Zakri, J. (2020, March 31). *What Is Sleep Hygiene? Plus 15 Tips for Better Sleep Hygiene.* Tuck Sleep.

https://www.tuck.com/sleep-hygiene/

Zimmerman, P. (2020). Photo of Woman Reading Book. In *Pexels*.

https://www.pexels.com/photo/photo-of-woman-reading-book-3747468/

LIVING WITH LOSS

FACING GRIEF AND ADVERSITY IN A SOCIETY
THAT DOESN'T UNDERSTAND

This book is dedicated to anyone facing the struggle of loss. You're not alone on this journey. It's time to challenge the status quo and create a better life.

INTRODUCTION

"It is better to conquer our grief than to deceive it. For if it has withdrawn, being merely beguiled by pleasures and preoccupations, it starts up again and from its very respite gains force to savage us. But the grief that has been conquered by reason is calmed forever. I am not therefore going to prescribe you those remedies which I know many people have used, that you divert or cheer yourself by a long or pleasant journey abroad, or spend a lot of time carefully going through your accounts and administering your estate, or constantly be involved in some new activity. All those things help only for a short time; they do not cure grief but hinder it. But I would rather end it than distract it."

— *SENECA*

As a young boy just entering my teen years, I lost my mother to a devastating battle with cancer. One day, she was raising me and giving me a great childhood. The next, I watched her deteriorate as she battled to the best of her ability. After she passed, the weight of her absence hit me like a freight train, and the grieving process quickly followed.

Through my adolescence and into my adult years, I realized that healing is not entirely linear. I would have moments of pure sadness, followed by feelings of rage or anger. On the days that I felt okay, I almost thought that I wasn't supposed to be happy. Above all, I was confused by what I was feeling and how long it lasted. I just wanted my mom back, and I wanted life to feel normal again.

After the loss of my mother, I was left feeling isolated from society. I allowed my sadness to rest deep inside my core, which caused me to become reclusive. There were times when I would not leave my house for days on end, even when my friends or family encouraged me to spend time with them. I felt all alone, though I knew that I had support within reach.

If you have picked up this book, you are probably feeling some of what I have felt. No matter who you are grieving or how long it has been, the loss of a loved one is arguably the most impactful life event you will experience. At times, the grief becomes unbearable to the point that it seems you cannot go on any longer. A life without your loved one is impossible to imagine.

This overwhelming sadness tricks you into thinking that this is your new normal and that happiness will never be achieved again. But this is not the case. Grief comes in stages, and it won't overwhelm you forever. Because each stage lasts for various lengths of time, you cannot predict an exact end date to your suffering, but you can feel confident in knowing that the next stage is coming. You will be able to get through it and heal.

Unfortunately, grief does not only appear in mental suffering. It causes physical symptoms that wear you down as well. The result is a powerful force that should not be underestimated or ignored.

But that doesn't mean you have to let it control your life. In this book, you will learn all of the tools you need to successfully acknowledge and process the grief you are experiencing. Even on the days when you feel that you are too overwhelmed with your emotions, you will figure out how to work through them by using the tips and methods in this book. You will also learn how to surround yourself with the best people in your life and find out ways to uplift yourself when you need an extra boost. This support will be vital to your healing.

Working through grief is a process. It is not something you should expect to handle overnight. Throughout your journey, you can expect to understand grief and how you can face the accompanying emotions, which is often one of the most difficult parts of healing. You will also learn:

- The physical and emotional symptoms of grief
- How to differentiate between grief and depression
- A detailed guide on the five steps of grief
- How to find solace in Stoicism
- How to face your pain directly

- How to deal with feelings of anger and rage
- The Wim Hof Method of dealing with grief

By the time you are through reading, you will feel like a weight has been lifted from you. You will have the ability to work through your feelings until you reach a point where you can celebrate the memory of your loved one who has passed.

I wrote this book because I understood that the way I felt when I lost my mother as a young boy is the way that a lot of people feel on a regular basis. Through years of research, I have come to understand the best ways to deal with loss. I hope for this book to guide you through all of the stages of grief as they come to you, and I believe that my research on the topic will assist you through them.

I have written another book titled *10 Habits for Grief and Loss: Create Change Through Adversity to Become a Better You* that details an abundance of healthy habits you can implement in your life to guide you through your grieving period. The goal of both books is to make you stronger both physically and emotionally. I am passionate about helping people, and I want to help you return to the person you once were before the grief entered your life.

By acknowledging your pain now instead of pushing it aside, you are one step closer toward acceptance and living a better life.

1

KNOW YOUR ENEMY

Grief is a powerful force to be reckoned with, yet you cannot see it in a tangible form. It weaves its way through you, getting tangled up in your emotions and thoughts. Most everyone will experience this pain at some point, but each individual will have a unique way of dealing with and processing grief. Some may begin the process right away, sorting through their anger, denial, and uncertainty. Others will need time to get there, often spending time mourning the loss until they reach a depressive state. Your version of grieving is not incorrect or wrong. You are feeling the loss, so you get to decide what you are going to do to mourn it.

The most important thing is to take care of yourself as you feel all of this intensity. Many people completely shut down after experiencing a loss because they feel it is too painful to go on. If you ever start to feel this way, stop for a moment to assess your situation. There are certain parameters that you can learn to better guide you on your path. Grief might not always look identical, but there are plenty of recognizable contributing factors that you can become aware of. By having this knowledge, you will be able to help yourself through even the most difficult times.

Remember that grief is completely natural, and you need to experience it before you can heal from the loss. Grief asks you to open up your mind, body, and soul to the fact that the person you love is now gone. It can be difficult to feel these things, especially when you are forced into the grieving process before you can fully comprehend what you are feeling. Take your time with it. If you try to rush, you aren't going to properly experience all of the emotions required to heal.

Grief can make you feel numb, causing you to withdraw from life and the things you normally love to do. Even simple tasks like going to the grocery store can feel too difficult or painful while you are grieving. Because it can be easy to deteriorate when you are not taking care of yourself, having a solid support system is crucial. You need to have some people who you are willing to let in as you sort through your emotions. This is a personal experience, so there should be no shame in asking for help during this time.

When you are working through the grieving process, it is best to fully let go of the idea that you are going to control it. There is no controlling mourning, and you end up being able to sort through it better when you stop trying. Instead, your focus should be on picking yourself back up and thinking about the things that will make you feel better.

Before you can get to that point, though, you need to understand what you are dealing with, which means understanding how grief works. In general, there are five stages of grief, which include the following:

- Denial
- Anger
- Bargaining
- Depression
- Acceptance

You might experience them in that exact order, or you might only feel one stage for a long time until you are ready to move forward. Do not pressure yourself into believing that you need to be further ahead than you are. By listening to your heart, you can figure out how long you must stay at each stage, even if they come out of order.

Grief is accompanied by mourning. Mourning can last for an undetermined amount of time. You might be processing the loss for weeks, months, or even years. All of these options are valid because you are going through something personal. Take as much time as you need to work through a difficult time. Make sure you surround yourself with all of the best resources to help you. If you ever feel uncertain about your process and if it is becoming detrimental to your life or well-being, you can always consult a medical professional for more guidance.

MYTHS ABOUT GRIEVING AND LOSS

To better understand the process of grieving a loss, it helps to recognize some of the most common myths. Through this knowledge, you will be able to validate your experience and get through it successfully.

Myth: Grief and mourning are the same.

You can think of your grief as a storage space for all of the thoughts and feelings that you have surrounding the loss of your loved one. Picture your grief like a big box that can be filled with all of the memories, photographs, experiences, and feelings that you had with this person. Some days, it can feel good to look back at all of the mementos you have collected along the way. On other days, thinking about your loved one can feel incredibly difficult. These feelings are intense because grief typically activates quickly once you discover you have lost a loved one. Your grief gives the loss an internal meaning that you will likely hold on to until you feel secure enough to move forward in your healing process.

While grief is made up of your internal feelings, mourning is the outward expression of those feelings. Mourning occurs when you decide to do something with the grief that you are holding on to. This means that you are ready to take your internal thoughts and feelings and express them in an outward fashion. This may include crying, which is a sign that you have begun mourning.

Other methods of mourning may include journaling, creating artwork based on the individual, talking about good memories you had with them, praying, and celebrating special dates that are relevant to that individual. Choose whichever one feels right to you.

To heal, you must reach the point of mourning because grieving is only going to keep your difficult feelings inside of you.

Myth: Women grieve more than men.

This notion likely stems from the idea that women tend to be more open and in touch with their emotions. In society, men are typically scolded or made fun of when they cry or express strong emotions. Therefore, it is thought that men are more hesitant to cry and get in touch with their grief because of these social constructs that have been in place for a long time.

In reality, grief does not discriminate, and both women and men can experience varying intensities when it comes to grief. Everybody deserves a chance to grieve properly regardless of gender identity. If you are a man who is going through the grieving process, remember that your feelings do not make you weak. Loss is a difficult subject to accept, and you need to do your best to reach this point.

To stop perpetuating this myth, it is necessary to support those who are grieving. Their experience might not make sense to you, just as yours might not make sense to others, but the support is going to make a big difference.

Myth: Not thinking about your pain will make it disappear.

This might work for a little while, but it is not a permanent solution. Instead, it leads to a stage called denial. Typically, this stage happens at the beginning of your grief, but it can enter again at any point.

When you live in denial, things might feel bearable. You stop thinking about your pain, so you stop feeling uncomfortable. Living in an ignorant state of mind makes it seem like you are healing without having to deal with the painful parts. What is often overlooked is the fact that this only suppresses emotions.

Eventually, they are going to come up again, often when you least expect them. And this time, they will be stronger because stifling your emotions makes them even more intense. While everything might feel okay on the surface, it only takes a small trigger to bring them back into the foreground of your life.

Although it is hard, it is best to experience your raw pain as soon as you can to fully process it. This is how you are going to make important steps toward being fully healed from the loss.

Myth: The first year is the hardest.

You will often hear people say that the first year after you lose someone is the hardest you have to experience. This puts the idea in your head that the years to follow are going to be easier. While the first year does have a particularly difficult feeling because you are going to be cycling through all of the holidays and special times of the year without this person, it does not necessarily become easier the next year. It might, or it might feel even more difficult because you are aware of all of the time that has passed.

You might experience several great years of making progress with the loss, only to feel derailed and back where you started in the first year. This is a normal part of the process, which is why it is so individual. You never know what you are going to experience, but going with the flow is going to allow you to navigate through it all. Do not put any pressure on yourself by falsely promising that the first year will be the worst. You do not know what might happen in the future, but this does not mean you should live fearfully. Take care of yourself as time goes on, and you will learn how to handle anything that comes your way.

Myth: Grief is a single emotion.

When you think about grief, you likely imagine sadness and tears. These can be big aspects of the grieving process, but they are not the only ones. Grief can take on many different appearances, some of which may surprise you.

Grief can come through as intense anger or rage, both for the situation and at the person lost. It can feel like confusion and being lost in a haze. You might also find yourself gravitating toward things that make you laugh or that make you happy because this is a defense mechanism against sadness.

No matter what you are feeling during your grieving process, be mindful of it. Never shame yourself for the way you feel because you cannot help this, just as you could not help that you lost someone you cared about. If you start to act out of character, understand that it might be the grief trying to get your attention. This can be an indication that you might be ready to start the mourning process and release your grief in an outward expression.

Myth: Grief is bad.

While grief *feels* bad, it is not inherently bad. You are going to have to process many difficult thoughts and feelings during this process, but the process itself is a positive one. Remind yourself that you have to work through these hard times to get to the point of happiness again. Only through recognizing your grief will you be able to find the path toward healing. If anyone tries to make you feel bad for the way you are grieving or the length of time you are grieving, they are not someone you need to keep close to you during this time.

Normalize grief because it is entirely natural. If you feel any kind of guilt or bad feelings about the way you are grieving, be easy on yourself. You are not doing anything wrong by exploring these feelings and trying to get to the bottom of them. You do not deserve to live with their burdens forever. It is brave to take an actionable step forward during your grieving process. Be proud of yourself for trying, even when you do not succeed right away.

Myth: There's a right way to grieve.

There is no standard or any rules when it comes to the way you experience grief. If anyone tries to tell you that you are doing it wrong or if you begin to second-guess yourself, remind yourself that it is an individualized experience. Only you know what it feels like to lose the loved one you did. Only you have the memories that you have with them, and you shared all of the experiences that you did. Your grief is not going to look the same as the grief of others, even if it is based on the loss of the same person. Human connections are so diverse, and only you know exactly what it felt like to be connected to the person you lost.

You will find a way that feels right for you, but this does not mean it is the only way. Since there are no rules in place, you get to try several different methods until you start to feel better. There is a lot of room for self-exploration in the process of grieving. You can take advantage of this by being willing to try different methods until you start to feel better. It might be incredibly difficult to take the leap, but it will prove to be worthwhile over time.

Myth: You can only grieve a death.

This is an interesting concept to explore. When people express that they are grieving, you probably jump to the conclusion that they have experienced a death. But grief can appear even when death is not involved. Losing something important to you can trigger symptoms of grief in the same way. The loss of a job is one example. If you get fired or laid off from the job that provided you with a stable income, you are placed in a position of loss that likely makes you feel uncertain. You might even feel like you are in denial in the beginning, and the anger will follow.

Losing a friendship due to betrayal is another instance when you might feel the need to grieve. Maybe a trusted person has proven to be untrustworthy, which is a jarring discovery to accept. You might become depressed from the devastation, and you will have to reach a point of acceptance before you feel okay about it. This is similar to the way you must move forward when you are grieving the death of a loved one.

Myth: Children do not grieve and should not attend funerals.

Much like any other individual, children can feel loss and grief in big ways. Their process might look different depending on how old they are and how well they can grasp the concept of death, but it is still grief. Allowing children the chance to express themselves during grief is so important. When they are not given any outlets for their grief, they can begin to internalize all of the anger and confusion, which can turn into detrimental mental health issues in the future.

Regarding funerals, this is a personal decision. A lot of children can grasp the concept of loss, and in some cases, a funeral might provide them with the necessary closure to help them make sense of the loss endured. This all depends on the child and how they are coping, but it is a good idea to observe their behaviors to determine if attending a funeral might put them at ease.

These are among the most common myths that circulate regarding grief. You have probably heard some of them before, and maybe you even believe them yourself. Now that you are learning more about the process, you can open your mind to new ideas surrounding grief and how to get through it.

PHYSICAL SYMPTOMS

When you are going through grief, you feel emotionally depleted. While this impacts your mind, it also impacts your body.

People going through grief often describe it as a debilitating illness. Not feeling your best physically tends to bring down your mood. Your body is also less capable of warding off illnesses because your immune system suffers. You need a certain amount of energy to function properly, and your grief can deplete this entirely.

Consider a study published in the journal *Ageing and Immunity*, which discovered that elderly people who have experienced the recent loss of a loved one were more at risk of developing infectious diseases (Romm 2014). When you are in so much emotional distress, you feel the heartbreak quite literally. This is why staying deep within your grief can be dangerous. Your body becomes weakened, susceptible to illness.

The last thing that you want to experience while you are mourning the loss of a loved one is the decline of your health. It is no secret that the older you get, the harder it is for your body to fight against potential illnesses. But what happens when age is combined with grief?

A study administered by the University of Birmingham's School of Sport observed two groups of mourners. One group had an average age of 32, while the other had an average age of 72. They used similarly aged control groups of individuals who had not experienced a recent loss. Throughout the study, the older mourners were found to have a weakened function in their neutrophils, which are the white blood cells found in the body that help fight against infections. While the younger group of mourners saw plenty of similar psychological symptoms, they didn't see the same physiological symptoms. Therefore, the study confirmed that those who are older are more biologically at risk of becoming ill after experiencing a loss (Romm 2014).

A further explanation of the above study states that there is a bigger difference between the older group of mourners and the younger group because of the stress hormone known as cortisol. By the time an individual reaches the age of 30, a person's DHEA levels drop. This is the hormone that typically balances your cortisol levels. With lower DHEA levels the older you get, the weaker your immune system becomes. Any exposure to prolonged depression or sadness due to a loss can become detrimental the older you are.

Aside from weakening your immune system, grief can take over other systems in your body that keep you healthy and functioning properly. When you are experiencing grief, you experience an increase in inflammation. In general, inflammation in any part of your body can become negative because it can worsen existing health problems and lead to new ones. When your body is constantly trying to fight against inflammation, its response system can start damaging healthy cells because it is being overworked. This is why you might experience different health problems that you've never had before.

The condition of your heart health is also worsened when you are experiencing grief. This is especially true if you are stuck in a cycle of grief for a prolonged time. Because of this, you are more prone to heart disease and high blood pressure. Some intense grief can even lead to a syndrome known as broken heart syndrome. This is a form of heart disease that appears similar to a heart attack, further proving how powerful the sadness of grief can become if not addressed properly. This is a scary ailment to experience because it can happen suddenly.

Through all of the physical distress, you are also more prone to develop panic attacks. Even though panic attacks usually occur due to mental triggers, they cause physical responses. Often, a panic attack includes increased heart rate, trembling/shaking, chills or hot flashes, tightness in your chest, and sweating. The panic takes over and convinces you that there is lingering doom ahead with nothing you can do to stop it.

The Common Link

As you navigate through your grief, the physical and emotional symptoms are connected by the stress you feel. When you are under a lot of stress, the systems in your body that control your physical and emotional stress are bound to overlap. As you are feeling more stressed out, your body is receiving signals to activate certain protective processes in your nervous system. In other words, your mind and body are working harder than ever. This is why it is easy to get sick when you are going through the process of mourning. Your stress can become chronic if left untreated, and this will cause you to rapidly deteriorate.

Many people are ashamed of the physical symptoms they feel because they do not want to appear weak or a burden. Remember that it is completely normal to be physically impacted by your grief. This does not make you an inconvenience to be around or a selfish person. Loss is difficult to comprehend and to address, so the way that you respond to it is often outside of your control. As you begin to move through the stages, you will learn how to process each symptom and take care of yourself again.

You may need reminders to practice self-care. When you are grieving the loss of a loved one, you are the last person that you are thinking about. All of the memories that you have with this person are likely occupying the space in your brain, and you often have little room to think about anything else. It can become easy to forget how to make yourself feel better or to even complete basic tasks, such as eating, sleeping, and showering. Before you get to this point of physical neglect, you must address all of the thoughts and feelings that you are having without judgment. You have every right to remember your loved one and to miss them, but you must remind yourself to stay on a safe path and to continue to take care of yourself in the process.

To keep yourself in check, consider the following physical symptoms of grief. If you notice them happening to you, they can serve as a sign to slow down and to take better care of yourself:

- Stomach pain
- Fatigue
- Chest tightness
- Decreased appetite
- Nausea
- Shortness of breath
- Dry mouth
- Headache

- Sweating

While these are not all of the physical symptoms you can experience, they are among the most common. Only you know how you are feeling physically, so you must pay close attention to these symptoms. If you feel that they are getting worse, it might be necessary to contact a medical professional for help. There is no shame in getting help during the process of mourning because it is a difficult one. Not everybody can navigate through it alone, and that is nothing to be ashamed of.

Remember that your biological makeup can also be an influential factor in this process. If you are older or already have physical ailments that you struggle with, then you are more susceptible to the physical symptoms of grief.

If you realize that you are experiencing these symptoms but do not require professional help, tune into them. Notice how your body feels and acknowledge why. This becomes an extension of your acceptance of the loss. Once you can identify your physical symptoms and understand that they are happening to you because of the grief, you can make a plan to heal from them and finally move forward in your process. Much like the emotional factors of grief, the physical factors also do not have a set timeline. You might feel bad for a few weeks, months, or years. It all depends on how your body processes the experience.

EMOTIONAL AND BEHAVIORAL CHANGES

If you feel that you haven't been yourself since the grief began, it is likely that your emotions and behaviors have been changing, which is common. While the process is different for each person, losing a loved one can trigger certain changes within that you might not recognize at first.

It can be alarming to one day notice that you are acting differently. You might also feel defensive when others in your life point out these changes. The best way to handle them if they start happening to you is to remain aware of them. By noticing any changes that you experience, you will have a better idea of what you need to do to heal from the grief and how to get through it in a healthy way. The below symptoms are explained to give you an idea of what you might be going through.

Anxiety

Anxiety can change a lot about your behavior. It can lead you to believe that something bad is going to happen to other loved ones in your life and maybe even cause you to question your mortality. When you experience anxiety, you have a worrying feeling that you cannot seem to shake. You might not be able to identify what exactly you are worried about, but the feeling can become persistent. There are plenty of instances that can trigger your anxiety that extend beyond thinking about the death of your loved one, which is why it can be tricky to realize that it is the cause.

Your anxiety triggers are personal, and they are valid. For example, if your loved one died in a car accident, you might find yourself triggered by something like the slamming of a car door.

You cannot help what triggers you, but you can get help with your anxiety. Focusing on your breathing and practicing meditation can become beneficial to you during this time. For any additional help, there is the option of speaking with a mental healthcare professional.

Detachment

This symptom is particularly common in the beginning stages of grief. Right after you lose your loved one, you are probably going to experience some degree of denial. Because of this, you will find it hard to stay in touch with the reality of your life. Everything is bound to feel distant and difficult to comprehend, even if it is an entirely normal part of your routine. For example, you might not experience the same enjoyment from spending time with people you care about or watching your favorite television show because your mind is elsewhere.

While it is not a good feeling to realize that you are detaching from your life, it usually fades over time. As you begin to heal from the loss, you will slowly start to feel joy and happiness again that you thought you lost permanently.

The thing to remember about grief is that no stage is permanent. While it can feel that this is going to be forever, understand that it will pass. Your brain needs time to comprehend what has happened and to find paths that you can take to work your way through it. Be patient and gentle with yourself if you find that you are now detached.

Loneliness

After losing someone you truly care about, the feeling of loneliness can set in. Even if you have a great support system around you, these individuals are not the person that you lost. It is okay if you feel that their presence is not the same because it should not feel the same. Acknowledge the uniqueness and special qualities of the individual you are grieving. This appreciation for them can bring forth positive memories that you can hold on to. While you are going through this process, be sure to acknowledge when other people in your life want to be there for you.

Even if you are not ready to be around people yet, you still likely have plenty who care about you in your life. They want you to be okay and want to support you through this difficult period. Grief can present the illusion that you are all alone or that you are the only one who feels this way, but it is not true. If you feel that you cannot talk to anyone in your life about what you are going through, consider meeting with a grief counseling support group. This will put you in contact with others who are experiencing the loss of loved ones. Knowing that others can relate to you in similar ways will help the feeling of loneliness dissolve.

Lack of Concentration

When you experience a loss, it often takes over every thought. You might be going over the situation constantly in your mind, leaving you unable to focus on anything else. It is not uncommon to have difficulty working or keeping up with your responsibilities during this time. Being preoccupied with the situation does not feel good, and it keeps your mood low because you are constantly reminded of the loss.

Finding healthy distractions will help you accept that it is okay to think about other things. You might feel that you do not deserve to feel happy during this time, but this is only a temporary feeling, much like the other symptoms that come with grief. You can read an uplifting book or surround yourself with people who have positive energy. Getting out of your head and out of the thoughts that plague you will help you refocus your concentration.

Sleep Disturbances

When you are emotionally distressed, your sleep is prone to interruptions. This can manifest in different ways, including insomnia. You might feel unable to sleep or too worried to fall asleep. This can happen because you are constantly thinking about the person you lost or the fact that they are gone. If you have been tossing and turning all night long, you are not going to feel rested in the morning.

If you can get to sleep, you might end up waking up a lot. With this kind of interruption, you are not getting the deep sleep that you require to feel rested. Being unable to reach your REM sleep might make you feel like you haven't slept at all.

There is also the possibility that you will experience an increase in nightmares that wake you up. The thoughts that you have before you fall asleep or the thoughts that are in your subconscious can impact what you dream about. Talking about your feelings will help you let go of these thoughts. With a clear mind, you will be able to finally rest again.

Troubling Thoughts

The thoughts you have while you are grieving might scare you or worry you. Because you are so focused on the loss of your loved one, you might experience thoughts that you never used to have before. Some people end up thinking about death a lot more or their health. This can become overwhelming if these troubling thoughts do not leave your head, and they can also contribute to any sleep disturbances that you might be having. When you are left to overthink situations, you are much more likely to hold on to these thoughts and let them bother you.

If you want relief from them, you can journal or talk to someone you trust. You might not feel comfortable expressing all of your deepest thoughts to someone in your life, even if you do trust them, but journaling can serve as a good outlet for you during this time. The best thing about journaling is that nobody has to ever read it. You can say anything that you want in an uncensored way to get all of your thoughts off your mind. Imagine them staying on the page as you write them down, clearing up space in your head for some peace of mind.

Restlessness

This is a common coping mechanism that tends to develop during grief. If you feel that you cannot sit still, you might be fighting avoidance. This stems from the denial stage of grief, and it can change your behavior in a powerful way without you realizing it. Immersing yourself in activities that take up a lot of time or energy might be a way for you to cope with the loss. There is a fine line between a healthy level of activity and doing so much that you are simply avoiding the situation at hand. If you constantly feel restless, this can be a sign that you need to slow down and address your feelings rather than keeping yourself busy.

Let yourself feel okay with remaining still for a few moments a day, even if this is when the upsetting thoughts come up. This might be necessary for you to successfully move toward your next stage of grief. It is going to feel uncomfortable, but this is how you are going to make improvements in your life. You can work through this process slowly, only allowing a little bit in at a time. There is no need to burden yourself by being consumed with these thoughts, but there must be a balance between distraction and stillness.

Loss of Appetite or Comfort Eating

Your gut health is directly connected to your mental health. When you feel nervous or stressed out, this can stimulate your appetite in different ways. Some people eat comfort foods when they feel uncomfortable. The food serves as temporary relief to the problem they are experiencing. But letting yourself indulge every day can become an unhealthy coping mechanism. The food that you eat becomes the fuel that gets you through each day. If you are consuming a lot of processed foods, fried foods, artificial ingredients, or sugar, then you are putting yourself at risk of developing physical ailments. It is okay to treat yourself to the things that you love once in a while, but make sure you are doing so to enjoy them, not to mask your feelings.

On the opposite end of the spectrum, you might experience an entire loss of appetite. Depression or sadness can usually trigger this symptom of behavior. You might feel that you are too upset to perform basic actions. This can include the act of caring for yourself by feeding yourself. With all of the sadness that you feel, you might not want to think about food during this time.

Understand that you need to keep yourself healthy if you want to make a full recovery, and eating during this time is essential. Do your best to make sure you are eating meals regularly, even if the portions are smaller. When you eat less but eat more nutritious food, you will get enough vitamins and minerals to keep yourself physically healthy.

If you have been experiencing any of the above changes, do not allow this to scare you or worry you. While you should get help if you feel overwhelmed by them, you can feel hopeful that you are moving through a normal cycle of grief. These changes indicate that your mind and body are both aware that you are going through something painful and difficult. What they are trying to achieve is adaptation.

2

THE THIN LINE BETWEEN GRIEF AND DEPRESSION

Many believe that grief and depression are the same. While you are mourning the loss of a loved one, you are going to be put into a state of severe sadness, which can often manifest into depression. The two do not always go hand in hand, however. In this chapter, you will learn the key differences between the typical cycles of grief and the indicators of depression.

Because depression can appear suddenly and bring an onslaught of dangerous side effects, it is important to recognize when it is happening. Depression often takes over in such a powerful way that you do not even realize you are in it. By knowing what to look for, you can ensure that you are taking all of the right precautionary measures to have the safest grieving period that you can.

Since both display similar symptoms, it can often be confusing to tell the difference between grief and depression. Another factor that makes each one difficult to differentiate is that they often overlap. When the two are so intertwined, it can be hard to see where one starts and one ends. Commonly, periods of extended grief will lead to depression. While this is not always the case, this seems to be one of the most common triggers for depression. The following similarities and differences will help you see what you should be looking for.

THE SIMILARITIES

As you read through each of these similarities, you will see that they can all define grief and depression in certain ways. By navigating through each one, determining the emotions that you feel and where they stem from, and gauging how long you have been experiencing them, you will be able to better understand if you are going through a typical cycle of grief or if you have developed depression. If it turns out that you are depressed, the outlook is not hopeless. You still have a chance to work through your grief in a healthy way.

Sadness

You are probably already pretty familiar with sadness. As you experience various events in your life, even those unrelated to loss or death, you will feel sadness. From the earliest instances of your childhood, you were taught what it meant to be sad, perhaps when your parents told you that you could not spend time with your friends or that you could not get that toy at the store that you had been eyeing.

As we age, we feel sadness for reasons that evolve. Through adolescence, you will likely move away from caring so much about material possessions or decisions that your parents make for you and, instead, shift your focus to your social circle and romantic interests. This is the next stage developmentally, and most of us can say that we experienced a heartbreak or two during those emotionally charged years. With all of the hormones circulating through our bodies, it is almost impossible to feel happy all of the time.

Then, as an adult, sadness usually dissipates. You learn how to deal with the fact that you cannot always get what you want and that things do not always work out as planned. While there is plenty that still can make you feel sad, you usually develop coping mechanisms to help you through the feeling. There are different ways you can do this, both unhealthy and healthy. Some examples of healthy coping mechanisms include venting to loved ones, journaling your feelings, and seeking therapy.

When your sadness is out of your control, unhealthy coping mechanisms tend to appear. You might try to fill the void with material items or dangerous behaviors that are out of character. Instant gratification becomes prominent during this stage because you simply want to feel happy again. Sadness is powerful, but what most do not realize is that it does not have to be overpowering.

How this relates to grief and depression is fairly straightforward. It lasts for a long time, and there is little that you can do to change the way you feel. In cases of sadness that are brought on by grief, this is a stage that you go through. While it can last for an extended period, you can find your way to the next stage. The sadness does not take over your entire life, and you can find outlets to express yourself during this time.

When your sadness comes from depression, getting through it feels a lot harder. Because you are so discouraged about getting past it, you remain in your depressive state. Then, the other symptoms start appearing. All of the things you used to love that brought you happiness no longer feel the same. It becomes impossible to simply "snap out" of your sadness because it is a lingering feeling that can often feel daunting, and it typically requires extra help to work through.

No matter where your sadness is stemming from, there is no need to feel ashamed because of what you are feeling. We all experience pain differently, and emotional pain is no exception. Be gentle with yourself as you try to work through all of your feelings that surround the passing of your loved one. This is necessary before you can move past your sadness. You must experience it, even if it is difficult.

Insomnia

A symptom that affects your sleep, insomnia might not seem like a big deal at first. It is common to become restless or even fearful at night because this is when your brain tends to focus on what is bothering you. As you begin to unwind each day, your mind will likely review all of the things that are on it. This is problematic when you have suffered a loss because grief can bring forward a lot of painful and surprising emotions that you might not be aware of that are lurking below the surface.

Experiencing the loss of a loved one can be triggering for many reasons. If you have lost someone in the past, this new loss might trigger the same feelings that you went through before. Since you remember how terrible it was to grieve that individual, your brain might put up certain barriers to not have to go through the same process again, even though you need to do this. It becomes easy to mentally block out certain memories and thoughts when your brain is trying to protect you from feeling pain.

You might become triggered because you start to feel fearful that you are going to lose other people in your life who you care about. This can even manifest into a fear of losing other important things, such as your job, house, or car. Anything important to you can get taken away, and this is not a comfortable thought to focus on when you are going through grief.

If you find yourself unable to sleep at night, you are probably experiencing insomnia because of one of the above reasons. Your mind starts racing, the fear kicks in, and you begin replaying all of the thoughts that make you feel sad, uncomfortable, or scared. Your brain just wants to keep this from happening, so it remains in a hyperactive state that prevents you from fully resting. This can go on for hours or even entire nights.

Without proper sleep, you are going to feel the impacts in your daily life. It is a lot harder to complete your responsibilities at work and home when you haven't slept at night. Your interactions with other people also become strained because you are more likely to be in a bad mood. Sleep is how you function successfully, and without it, you are going to start acting differently.

It is normal to experience insomnia for a short amount of time when you are going through the loss of a loved one. This is likely to happen during the beginning of your process, and it will usually taper off as you begin to heal from the loss. If it persists for an extended time, this can be an indication that it is happening due to depression. The feeling is usually chronic when you are depressed and unable to sleep. It can also feel more intense.

Make sure that you are taking inventory of your mental health closely. If you notice that your lack of sleep is debilitating, then there is likely a need for intervention. There are many ways that you can guide yourself through this symptom, even if you do not seek therapy. By doing something relaxing before bed, such as yoga, reading a book, or drinking hot tea, you can put your mind at ease to the best of your ability. There are also natural remedies that you can take, like Melatonin, that promote that sleepy chemical in your brain.

Poor Appetite

One of the first signs of grief and depression you will notice is your lack of appetite. With both, the feeling hits you instantly because you will start refusing meals that you normally eat. What you eat to fuel your body is important normally, but this is especially true when you are going through a loss. The vitamins and nutrients you get from fueling your body with healthy foods make you feel physically stronger. Without them, you are going to deteriorate a lot faster.

Even if you are still eating, changing the portion size suddenly is still going to impact you because your body is used to eating a certain amount each day. This can lead to feelings of lethargy, laziness, or dizziness. The longer you experience this symptom, the more dangerous it can become. There are even some instances where your lack of appetite can trigger eating disorders, which seem like they will help you because you can be in control of what you are or are not putting into your body.

Be easy on yourself when you first notice that your appetite is not the same. You are processing a lot of new information and adjusting to life without a person who was important to you. Even when you do not feel like eating, try to encourage yourself to have meals that are small and packed with protein. While you might not be eating as much as you used to, having these smaller portions is better than not having anything at all.

With grief, this symptom should subside fairly quickly. You will feel it dissolve, much like insomnia, over time.

If you notice that it is not going away and that you are not eating at all, then this might be an indication that you are struggling with a bigger problem due to depression. Since depression can be chronic, so can your lack of appetite. You might find yourself going for several hours or even days without food. This is going to impact you both physically and mentally. When you are not refueling your body regularly, you are going to be running off of the little energy you have from sleeping.

Thinking about this one step further, if you are not sleeping, there is not much fuel that you are providing for your mind and body. Simple tasks are going to feel a lot harder and more overwhelming to accomplish. This can make you even more depressed as you see that you are unable to do the things that you used to do before. It becomes a difficult and dangerous cycle that can be hard to free yourself from.

The people you surround yourself with during this time are going to make a big impact on your recovery whether you are experiencing grief or depression. If you keep the people who care about your well-being close to you, they will be there to remind you to take care of yourself and to help you get enough nutrition throughout your days.

It is surprising how the influence of those around you can truly help you because you will start to mirror their behavior. It is no surprise, though, that those you spend the most time with become a part of you in many ways. Their habits and personality traits are bound to rub off on you because you are around each other so much.

Weight Loss

This symptom directly relates to your loss of appetite. Because you are not consuming as many calories as before, you lose weight as you cycle through the grieving process. This weight loss can happen quickly, but it should eventually plateau. Just as you will start to regain your hunger and be able to get a good night's sleep again after some time, you should also start to regain any weight that has been lost as you were mourning. This is an indication that you are following a path of grief.

When you are depressed, the weight falls off quickly and easily. A lot of people are shocked to see that they might still be eating, yet the number on the scale keeps getting lower. This can impact you in many different dangerous ways. Weight loss due to depression can either hinder your self-esteem or excite you because of the unintentional results that you see. An individual might feel embarrassed that they have lost so much weight, becoming a shell of who they used to be. Feeling physically weak can also lead to more emotional weakness.

You may be on the other end of the spectrum and excited by the weight loss. This is a symptom that is trying to turn into an unhealthy coping mechanism. With all eating disorders and related disorders that often stem from depression, the main topic is control. When you see yourself losing weight because you are not eating as much as you once were, you feel that you can control something happening to you in your life. Since you were unable to control the loss of your loved one, this makes you feel better because it acts as a placeholder for all of the control that you thought you had lost permanently.

When you are grieving and depressed, your mind will grasp at any other habits, thoughts, or behaviors to focus on other than the painful reality that you are left to face. Becoming too involved with your recent weight loss can get dangerous quickly. It is important to accept help when it is offered to you or to reach out to someone if you can see that the symptom is becoming too much for you to bear. Other people in your life are probably going to take notice of this physical change, and it is hard to listen to their advice when it is only going to sound like criticism to you.

Open your mind to the idea that these people just want to help you because they care about your well-being. They do not want to see someone they love deteriorate in front of their eyes. With depression, you might not be able to care about this and will continue on your path without food. An intervention is often necessary because this ends up putting you at risk of physical harm. Your body will start to shut down if you stop feeding it, and this is going to debilitate you for obvious reasons.

There are always resources that you can seek if you feel too embarrassed to accept help from the people in your life. Your health and mental health are both so important, and you should never feel ashamed if you reach a point where you admit that one or both are out of your control. There are ways that you can get your life back on track without putting yourself in dangerous positions.

THE DIFFERENCES

There are a few key differences between grief and depression. Below, you are going to explore them so you can become familiar with what each one looks like. By having this awareness, you are taking an additional step toward your healing by ensuring that you are being as safe as possible.

Diagnosis

When you are experiencing a normal phase of grief, you are not officially diagnosed with an illness or an ailment. While you know that grief can take a major toll on your life, it is a normal response to have when you discover you have lost someone you care about. As you are going through grief, all of the symptoms that come with it are going to assist you during your healing. As you cycle through each stage, you will learn how to become stronger and how to successfully manage your grief. In the long run, you are going to learn how to turn your grief into a healing experience.

Before you can feel like you are back to normal, you must explore all of the elements of your grief and where it takes you. While this might be difficult and uncomfortable in many ways, it is encouraged that you explore these feelings as much as you can. When you can get to the bottom of your emotions, you will have a better idea of how you can process them.

This is the foundation for grief and grieving. Since it is a process, you already know that it can take any given amount of time. This is where things can become unclear as to whether you are experiencing normal grief or whether you are going through depression. As time goes on, you may start to wonder if what you are feeling is still falling in line with the typical cycles of grieving.

It is important to check in with yourself often. Understand how you are feeling and why. Consider if any of your symptoms are debilitating you in any way. You do not need to completely stop working or eating to be impacted by your grief. Debilitation can come in the form of ignoring other responsibilities or important regular tasks, such as keeping up with cleaning your house or showering each day. Neglecting habits that keep you healthy and safe could be an indication that your grief is evolving into something further like depression.

While you are grieving, do not stress yourself out by constantly analyzing your behaviors. You do want to monitor them, but not in a way that is going to make you feel overwhelmed or uncomfortable. Be as open and honest with yourself as possible. This is why it is essential to let your thoughts and feelings out through a healthy coping mechanism. When you can unleash what is on your mind, you will be able to better analyze if you are simply going through grief or if you are developing a depressive disorder that is proving to be hard to manage.

No matter how bad each stage of grief gets, you should generally feel that you have everything under control. While your life might feel as though it is spiraling, deep down, you know that it is not. You understand that this is only a temporary part of your life and that you will successfully make it through. Understanding this indicates that you have a healthy grasp on your healing process and that you should cycle through the stages of grief successfully.

Depression is a diagnosed condition. You can find it in the *Diagnostic and Statistical Manual, Volume V* (DSM V). This is the guide that mental healthcare professionals use to diagnose their patients. According to the manual, some of the most common symptoms of depression include:

- Worthlessness
- Extreme guilt
- Suicidal thoughts
- Low self-esteem
- Powerlessness
- Helplessness
- Agitation
- Loss of interest in pleasurable activities
- Exaggerated fatigue

You might feel a lot of these symptoms as you are grieving, but they do not last for an extended period. If the problems you face are ongoing, then this might be an indication of something more serious taking place. The only way to get an official diagnosis for depression is to consult a professional. It is not wise to self-diagnose because this can cause your symptoms to become exaggerated due to worry. Still, you need to pay attention to the way you are feeling, especially if you have recently been having thoughts of suicide.

Another difference between depression and grief is that depression can be dangerous. If you are continually feeling so low, your life might be in jeopardy. Depression causes you to become unable to think clearly, only focusing on what is upsetting you. When this happens to someone who is also grieving, the difficulty can feel like too much to bear. This is why people will often think about suicide as a way to end the pain and suffering. It might seem easier to be gone than to have to deal with the reality of your loved one being gone. No matter what is going on in your life, suicide is not the answer.

If you begin to feel the above symptoms for an extended period, talk to someone. Even if you do not feel that it will help you, reaching out to someone is necessary during this time. Knowing that you are not alone can help to lift you out of the hole you feel that you are in right now, as can psychotherapy. Of course, a mental healthcare professional needs to evaluate you before establishing the best treatment plan.

When you are depressed, your daily routine will often seem incredibly difficult for you to complete. From dropping the kids off at school to getting your work done, this can seem like a hard thing to ask of you during this time. When you think about the loved one you have lost and you have depression, you might be met with feelings of emptiness. This usually occurs because your brain is trying to protect you from the pain of their loss. Instead of being able to look back on warm memories with this person that you cherish, you can only suppress them until you no longer feel anything. Instead of reminding yourself about the good times you had, your brain begins to attack your psyche.

If you have depression, you should not feel ashamed, weak, or unstable. Depression forms due to a chemical imbalance in your brain. Because you are physically unable to give your brain the necessary hormones it needs to feel happy, it takes on sadness instead. Depression is difficult to fight, but you can get through this. If you have been diagnosed with depression or you feel that you would like to talk to someone about it, remember that you are not alone.

Depression is not something that typically resolves itself like grief will. It is a mental illness that has the likelihood of getting worse before it gets any better. Your depression is often going to look like a downward spiral until it feels like it is too overwhelming to bear. If you have any doubts about whether or not you are experiencing depression or regular grief, it is a good idea to talk to someone about what you are going through.

Persistence

As you now know, grief is something that will usually resolve itself over time. You are still going to cycle through its stages, and some of them will be challenging and uncomfortable, but this is normal, and you can work through it. As you experience different feelings and emotions, you learn how to cope with the loss of the one you love to get back to a functional version of your life. This does not mean you are forgetting about them or "moving on." You can still fondly remember your loved one while also living a successful life.

You might feel like it is not okay to be happy while you are grieving, but think about the life you still have left to live. Consider how everything changed in an instant for the person that you lost and how they would probably want you to continue to live your life to the fullest. No day is ever a guarantee, so you need to make the most of each one while you still can. Grief isn't always going to feel this simple, but this is the goal that you should be aiming for, all while focusing on your emotions and working through them with healthy coping mechanisms.

During the first few weeks, you might not feel any different. It might even become apparent that nothing has changed with the way you feel. This is normal. Most people do not feel a shift until they have been grieving for some time. One day, you are going to wake up and realize that it is okay to be happy again. You are going to fondly remember your loved one and the time that you got to spend with them instead of dwelling on the fact that you have lost them. While it won't be easy, the process will teach you how to calm yourself down and refocus your energy on happier thoughts.

Healing happens in waves. You might feel like you are getting a lot better, only to experience a bad day where you feel that you are right back at the beginning of your grieving. This is also normal and happens because healing isn't linear. You might have bad days even years from now, but you will get through them, just like you got through your loss. The best way to make sure that you grieve as long as you need to is by listening to your feelings. If you feel like there are unresolved emotions that you need to address, do so gently. Be kind to yourself as you work on navigating through them and potentially getting the help that you need.

When you have depression, you might also have good days and bad days. The difference here is that you are still depressed daily. No matter how good your day is, there is still a lingering feeling of sadness that won't go away. You might feel like you are running away from your pain and sadness, only for it to catch up with you eventually. There is also the possibility that you will go through measures of distracting yourself or seeking out unhealthy coping mechanisms to feel less sad.

Just because the issue is out of sight does not mean that it is out of mind. If you suppress your feelings, they are bound to come back to the surface at any given time. It might take a small trigger for you to realize that you have yet to process any of your grief and that you must start from the beginning. Depression is great at masking your true feelings because it causes you to become numb. No matter how hard you try, you might still find that you are not getting to the real root of the problem.

Your depression can become persistent, nagging at you daily. Even if you only feel it in small ways, these will add up a lot over time. Everything from the way you talk, act, and think will be impacted by your depression if you allow it to completely take over your life. It is a mental illness that thrives on persistence and longevity. You can feel depressed for so long that you end up believing this is your new normal. But life does not have to feel this way any longer. There is hope, and there are resources you can use to get help.

There tends to be a stigma that surrounds talking to a therapist and getting help for your mental health because physical health is usually made a priority. Just because you cannot see a cut, scrape, or bruise does not mean you aren't in pain. Your mental health matters just as much as your physical health, and you should take it seriously despite what anyone else might think about you.

Nobody else gets to tell you how to heal or what to do regarding your mental health. It is a personal decision for you to make because only you know what you are going through. While depression might be a constant in your life at the moment, you will find ways to work through it and to replace it with other fulfilling elements. You will no longer feel dependent on your sadness, and you will finally be able to live a life that is free of the hardship that your depression has put you through. No matter who you lost or how long ago they passed, depression does not discriminate. It can appear when you least expect it, causing you a lot of mental strain. Be easy on yourself during this time.

While depression is sometimes inevitable during this process, this does not mean you need to feel discouraged or upset with yourself. So many people struggle with their mental health, even those who are incredibly strong. Admitting that you have a problem does not make you weak, nor should it make others think any less of you. If you feel that you are in over your head, there are ways to correct this problem and get your life back on track after you experience your grief.

COMPLICATED GRIEF SYNDROME (CGS)

There are instances where your regular grief can transform into something more severe known as complicated grief syndrome or CGS. The main difference between regular grief and CGS is that the latter is acute and can cause long periods of suffering for the person going through the loss. Some medical professionals suggest that CGS stems from an attachment disorder, which is what happens when you have an intense and long response to a stressor. In the past, doctors avoided treating people who displayed signs of CGS because it was technically a subcategory of grief. While not everybody experiences it, the result is usually still one that ends in healing.

Today, doctors look at CGS differently. Since CGS closely resembles a disorder, they are more willing to look into treatment options for those who cannot withstand their symptoms. Doctors used to view grief as a personal matter that did not necessarily require medical treatment, but through CGS, they are now discovering that it can make you feel similar to depression. You might experience feelings of worthlessness or helplessness, even becoming suicidal. CGS can be dangerous, and it should always be taken seriously.

Some symptoms of GCS include:

- Powerful pain at the thought of your lost loved one

- Heightened focus on reminders that you have lost a loved one
- An overall feeling of numbness
- A feeling of bitterness
- A loss of purpose/motivation
- A loss of trust in other loved ones

If these symptoms last for months after you have lost your loved one, you likely need to seek medical help from a professional.

Looking at these symptoms, some of them resemble what you typically experience as you go through grief. They can also mirror certain depression symptoms. A difference with CGS is that the pain leaves you in a hyper-alert state of being. There are lows, but there can also be intense periods of emotion (bitterness and loss of trust). The moods you experience while going through CGS are more up and down than regular grief or depression.

Even if you are experiencing both CGS and depression symptoms, these are two different ailments that must be treated differently. Many people are quick to assume that it is just one or the other or maybe that something is a normal part of grief. You know yourself better than anyone, and you know how you feel deep inside. If you have any inkling that something is not right, tell someone. Seek help before you are overcome by your sadness. It is never too late to ask for help, even if you have been experiencing these symptoms years after your loved one has passed.

If you do end up being diagnosed with CGS, understand that this does not mean your chances of feeling better have diminished. You might just have to take some additional steps to get there. You cannot control if you develop the syndrome or if you follow a more standard path of grief, so you should never punish yourself for the way that you must heal.

Healing is personal, so never compare your journey to someone else's. Each one is different, and neither is wrong.

3

THE FIVE STAGES OF GRIEF EXPLAINED

To better understand the grief you are going through, it helps to take a look at a model created by Dr. Elisabeth Kübler-Ross, author of *On Death and Dying*. Her influential work, which was inspired by her time with dying patients, has helped many to understand both the five stages of grief and the feelings of those who are about to pass on. While the Kübler-Ross model of grief was first introduced in 1969 when there were few resources on the subject, it is still relevant today.

I will be touching more on this in the coming chapter but although these stages are a great guide, grief is a very personal experience and it can be unpredictable. Don't be dependent on the stages and know that the structure will most likely vary from person to person. Just be open to each stage and be gentle on yourself if things aren't moving as quickly as you intend.

THE STAGES

These stages of grief have already been mentioned briefly, but this chapter will further break down each step according to the Kübler-Ross model. This model was created to help those who were dying to cope with the reality of the situation and was meant to ease the process and help them feel at peace with letting go. The model was then used to help the family members and loved ones of the person who had passed on. Many refer to these stages by the acronym DABDA.

Denial

"This is a mistake."

When you first find out about the loss of your loved one, it is common to refuse to believe the information because it is so shocking and upsetting. This is a defense mechanism that protects you from feeling sad. When you are in this period of disbelief, you usually do not mourn or show much outward emotion because you truly cannot comprehend the loss.

Although you are in denial outwardly, your brain is trying to process the information you were just given. It is cycling through all of the possibilities, like if the news is true or not, and working in overdrive to attempt to make sense of it all. This denial stems from the inability to be fully prepared for a loss. In some cases, you might have a loved one in your life who is terminally ill, but even then, you cannot predict the exact moment when you will lose them.

A common misconception is that you should prepare for the death of your loved ones before they happen to avoid the denial stage. Remember, though, that the stage of denial is necessary and normal to experience. If you try to skip this stage, you will inevitably come back to it in the future. The best thing you can do is to enjoy your life and your time with your loved ones. When a loss does occur, let your brain respond naturally. You might be in denial for a time, but this will soon pass.

Denial ends when you realize that they are truly gone. It might take a visit to the person's home or attending their funeral to fully realize this. When you do reach the point where you can see that you've been in denial, do not punish yourself. You cannot control how your brain reacts to stimuli, and it was simply trying to protect you. What you can do is focus on moving forward to the next stage of grief. You are about to deal with the bulk of emotions that have risen to the surface.

Anger

"This is unfair!"

Reaching the anger stage of grief is an indication that you have accepted the loss. However, this does not mean that you have worked through all of the emotions surrounding it. Anger is usually the next emotion that surfaces because it is a strong emotion. You do not want to give in to the sadness that threatens to take over because you have lost your loved one, so instead, you resort to anger.

The anger that you feel will not necessarily manifest in the way that you think it might. It may be targeted toward yourself, blaming your presence or lack of presence for the loss. You might wish that you had done more or spent more time with your loved one. It is common for regrets to form during this stage.

The anger may also be directed toward other people in your life. Even if they have done nothing wrong and have nothing to do with the loss of your loved one, you might still find it easy to unintentionally take it out on them. Because you know that you have people in your life who love you unconditionally, there is usually no fear that they will leave you. Therefore, it becomes easy to subconsciously take your anger out on them. This can manifest in the way you speak and behave. You might be harsher than usual and less pleasant to be around because of it.

There is another unique way that your anger can appear: anger at the person who passed away. Though they are no longer here, it is normal to be mad at them for passing away. This can be a conflicting feeling because you are sad that they are gone, but you also feel intense anger over that. You understand that it wasn't their choice, but you still feel mad that it happened.

Bargaining

"If only they hadn't gotten into the car."

The bargaining stage of grief is like the "what if" stage. You begin to question if things would have gone differently if your loved one had made different choices. You might even question what you could have done differently to prevent their passing. Deep down, you probably already know that nothing you could have said or done would have saved them, but it is still an overwhelming sensation to think about the possibilities. This is especially true if the loss was traumatic or accidental. Death always teaches us that you never know what is going to happen and when. Life can be so unpredictable, sometimes in jarring ways.

If you believe in a higher power, you may bargain with them. You might pray that they take this news back in exchange for you being a better or more devoted person. While you know that this is not how life and death work, you still desperately try anything you can to revoke the bad news you received.

Bargaining is similar to denial, but there is action involved. You are actively trying to stop the news from being true, and you are willing to make changes or think about other possibilities. This stage of grief can cause you to act differently in an attempt to remedy the situation.

There is no telling how long you will be in the bargaining stage or when it will appear, but remind yourself that you must be willing to let go of the things you cannot control. If you stress over factors that are far outside of your control, you are going to become sick with worry and stress. Letting go is hard, but this does not mean you are letting go of your loved one or the memories that you have of them. By understanding that you are not in control of any one person's mortality, you can move forward in your mourning process.

Depression

"My reason for living is gone."

While you have learned a lot about depression as a mental illness, it also exists as a normal stage of grief. As you already know, the difference is typically within the longevity of the symptoms. Your depression during grief might last for a long time as sadness is a prominent emotion. However, it should start to dissipate over time. You should be able to notice a difference in the way you are feeling, and ultimately, the time that passes will allow you to heal.

However, while you are in the depression stage of grief, life might feel like it isn't going to be okay ever again. At this point, reality has fully set in. You know that your loved one is gone and that there is nothing you can do to change this. All of the emotions that were once bottled up during the earlier stages are now able to come out. This can result in a lot of sadness and emptiness. You might feel that there is a physical space that is missing from within due to the loss of your loved one. This sadness can quickly lead to depression in the form of a mental illness if you do not take care to check in with yourself.

No matter how long this stage lasts for you or how many times you return to it during your grieving, accepting that you feel down is going to help you get through it. You have just lost someone important to you, and it is not realistic to expect yourself to put on a brave face. Loss is scary, hard, and uncertain. It is okay to feel that you are not okay right now. What will get you through this time is knowing that you can heal and feel okay again. This is not forever, and anything that impacts you to such a degree is bound to make you stronger in the long run.

Acceptance

"They are gone, and I miss them."

Reaching the point of acceptance does not automatically mean that you no longer feel sad or upset that your loved one has died. Instead, it means that you have cycled through your emotions and come to the conclusion that you must continue to live your life, even if you still miss and remember them every day. Because accepting their passing does not mean that you need to push their memory aside, your life can be abundant and still full of all of the wonderful times that you spent together. There will be moments when the sadness comes back, but this should not last for too long.

It is okay to cry if you feel like crying, even if you feel that you are at the acceptance stage. Cycling through grief does not mean you are losing any progress. Instead of feeling like you are going backward, acknowledge what you are feeling and try to get to the bottom of it. Often, certain events can trigger you into cycling through the stages. For example, if you wake up feeling extra sad on this person's birthday, you might end up thinking about them and how angry you are that they are not around to celebrate. This is completely normal, and it will probably happen on more than one occasion. Still, you have reached acceptance because you understand the reality of the situation.

Acceptance does not always feel good, but it can lead you to moments that do feel good by honoring and remembering your loved one in the best way possible. At this stage, talking about them usually brings you more joy than sadness or anger. Your mood swings will have leveled out by this point, and you will start to feel more stable. Since dealing with a loss can impact every area of your life, you will slowly start to see things return to normal. You will be able to work through your usual routines with no problems, and everything will fall back into place, as it should.

OTHER GRIEF MODELS

The Kübler-Ross model is not the only model for dealing with grief. After Kübler-Ross passed away, other experts came forward to further expand on the grief model, even making their own. Some prominent researchers who released their information include John Bowlby and Murray Parkes. Bowlby's Attachment Theory and Parkes's Four Stages of Mourning are still widely recognized today, much like the Kübler-Ross model.

Bowlby's Attachment Theory

John Bowlby was a British psychologist and psychoanalyst who was credited with creating his attachment theory. This theory surrounds the idea that the attachments we make early in our lives impact us well into adulthood. Bowlby believed that these attachments influence our mental and developmental health. With the help of fellow psychologist Mary Ainsworth, he came up with this theory that explains the various attachment types and why they form.

Overall, Bowlby believed that children are biologically programmed to seek out and remain close to attachment figures, such as their parents and guardians. When they are close to these individuals, they are given comfort, guidance, and nurturing. These figures are somewhat responsible for the child's survival, and by staying close by, the child knows that they are dependent on them.

During his early work, Bowlby worked with children. He was mainly interested in the subject of child development and what would happen if the child was taken away from their caregiver. He wanted to see how this would impact the child's developmental health.

His definition of attachment was that the child and the parent shared "lasting physical connectedness." Bowlby firmly believed that all babies need this type of bond with a caregiver starting in the infant stage because it increases the child's ability to survive. Because babies are born with the ability to cry and coo, Bowlby also believed that caregivers were programmed to naturally respond to these cues. For example, if a baby is crying, the caregiver will pick them up to soothe them.

Even though parents are typically seen as the primary caregivers in an infant's life, there are other attachment figures that this logic applies to. Whether it is another family member or a close family friend, if the infant grows up knowing this person, they have a chance to form a close bond with them. Anyone who provides security and comfort can become an attachment figure in the baby's life.

Bowlby made sure to note that feeding was not one of the reasons for bonds to form. Even without feeding the baby, which is still necessary for survival, you can become an attachment figure by simply providing that feeling of safety and security.

The following are the stages in which attachment forms, according to Bowlby's theory:

1. **Pre-Attachment**: Babies recognize their primary caregiver(s) at this stage. However, they have not yet formed an attachment to them. As they start to learn how to live in

the world by crying and fussing to express themselves, the attentiveness of their caregiver(s) will show them what love and nurturing is. This is a rewarding experience for both the little one and the parent(s). This stage continues until the baby is around three months, then they recognize their primary caregiver(s) in a way that feels secure and trusting.

2. **Indiscriminate Attachment**: Infants begin to show a preference for their primary caregiver(s) at this stage. They might only be soothed while crying when a parent or guardian tends to them. Even if other adults in their life are capable of the same kind of care, the bond already exists with the primary caregiver(s). That is not to say that the infant will not form close bonds with other caregivers in their lives. If a person is a constant in their lives, they will take a liking to them as well. Trust will be formed on a secondary level to the primary caregiver(s).

3. **Discriminate Attachment**: At this stage, the child has preferences as to whom they trust and wish to be around. They have a strong bond with their caregiver(s), and if they become separated, they might even experience some separation anxiety because they are nervous that they do not know when their caregiver is coming back. An example of this would be when a parent puts their child in daycare because they have to go to work. The child might have a hard time adjusting at first because they are not with their usual caregiver, and they might become fussy and cranky until they can be reunited.

4. **Multiple Attachment**: The child is growing up, but they

still hold a preference for their primary caregiver(s). This is an explorative stage where the child will take an interest in getting closer to other adult figures in their lives. This can be a teacher, a family friend, or other relatives. If those figures are around the child enough, a bond will form that slightly mirrors the bond of the primary caregiver(s). Because the child was introduced to nurturing and care as an infant, they know how to form bonds with other adults in their lives as they grow up.

Thinking about this differently, what might happen if a baby grows up without enough care? Unfortunately, neglect occurs. If a baby is not picked up when they cry or is not cared for when they soil their diaper, they learn that nobody is going to tend to them when they are in distress. The baby will likely grow up with a distrust of adult figures in their lives, even possibly extending to a distrust of other people when they are adults. Their bonds with their caregivers are not strong, and the feeling becomes mutual.

Extreme neglect does not have to be present for a child to lack in this developmental region. In some cases, a baby simply may not take to a parent. Fortunately, there are ways that this can be fixed. The parent might need to spend more time with the baby while being more attentive. Skin-to-skin contact can also create a moment of bonding that cannot be duplicated after the child is out of the pre-attachment stage.

Bowlby's theory suggests that your earliest attachments create the framework for the rest of your life. This is why early childhood development became his passion. He understood that the bond needs to happen sooner rather than later. Otherwise, it becomes more difficult.

The Four Patterns of Attachment

You might be familiar with a term known as "attachment style." It is used for both children and adults and refers to the way you bond with other people in your life. According to Bowlby's theory, this pattern is likely to stay with you if it is the one you grew up with.

Understanding your attachment style can teach you a lot about how you manage your grief and how you experience loss. It further proves that some things are outside of your control, but you can learn to work with them.

Here are the four patterns:

1. **Ambivalent**: This type of attachment happens when a child is distressed after a parent leaves. The separation anxiety impacts them in a debilitating way because their primary caregiver is unavailable. It is a fairly uncommon attachment style to maintain. However, if a child grows up knowing that a parent is too busy to care for them or does not seem to prioritize them, they have a hard time trusting and relying on other people as adults.

2. **Avoidant**: As the name suggests, children with this attachment style tend to avoid their caregivers. They have no preference between one or the other, and they treat a stranger the same way. This is usually the result of abuse or neglect. Because they were shown early on that the primary

figures in their lives are not going to care for them or keep them safe, the children become distrustful of everyone around them. To deal with this, they typically avoid asking for any help or advice. In adults, this attachment style comes off as independent at first glance. On the inside, however, the person might want to reach out but does not know how or is afraid of rejection.

3. **Disorganized**: This is probably the most confusing of the four attachment styles. A child will appear disoriented or confused, and there might be some avoidance or resistance of the primary caregiver(s). It is usually an indication that the child did not properly bond with the parent(s). While they might still provide the child with security and work on nurturing them when they can, there is a slight disconnect in the way that the child feels about them. This is why the behavioral pattern can read in many different ways. In adults, the person might be hard to get close to or make impulsive decisions regarding their social or romantic lives because they do not know how to follow a set attachment pattern.

4. **Secure**: A secure attachment type is the one to strive for. This looks like a child becoming distressed when separated from their parent(s) and feeling joy once they are reunited. When distress is involved, it is not debilitating as it would be in an ambivalent attachment, and there is a balance where the child understands who cares for them and that they have someone they can rely on in their lives. They know that their caregiver(s) will come back for them if they have to be apart. With a secure attachment style, the child feels comfortable

seeking guidance and nurturing from their caregiver(s). This makes for an adult who knows how to express themselves and what they need.

The attachment types further showcase the importance of forming healthy bonds with caregivers at a young age. Since these patterns begin at birth, caring for a child will shape them for the rest of their lives. If you feel that you have developed a negative or difficult attachment style, you can now see that this is not your fault. Everything that happened to you began before you had any autonomous control.

Parkes's Four Stages of Mourning

Bowlby's Attachment Theory was not centrally focused on grief. While it can explain a lot about the human psyche, it is more of an indicator of how early childhood development impacts you as you reach adulthood. It was only later when Bowlby's work caught the attention of grief psychologist Dr. Murray Parkes that a model emerged that was grief-centered. This model is known as the Four Stages of Mourning or the Four Phases of Grief. The foundation of this model is surrounded by the idea that attachment is broken when you lose a loved one. The way you react after this happens is a natural human response and includes:

Shock and Numbness: You can expect these two feelings immediately following the loss of a loved one. Parkes's model suggests that this occurs because you are not yet ready to process the death or accept that it happened. Like the denial stage when talking about the standard model of grief stages, you become keen on protecting yourself from the pain of the loss. This defense mechanism is triggered with little warning, and you often have to sort through it for a while before you can move on to the next stage.

What your mind needs is instant gratification. Understandably, a loss is painful and shocking, and your brain does not want to feel this pain, even for a minute. You may be left unable to cry, which is completely normal because you can't process your emotions. You remain shocked and numb until something breaks you down, allowing you to experience your true feelings.

Again, there is no set amount of time that you will stay in this stage. People cope with loss differently, so the responses are diverse. You cannot force yourself to feel a certain way if you simply do not, so try not to be hard on yourself if you think you are not mourning in the same way as those around you. This is a personal experience, and it is going to be treated as such. You need to do what you can to come to terms with the loss on your own time. Cry if you feel like it, remember the person if you feel like it, and openly discuss it if you feel like it. There should not be too much pressure placed on your shoulders in the beginning; it will only make you feel more resistant to the end goal of acceptance.

Yearning and Searching: This is a time when you likely feel lost and baffled that this could happen to the person you love. The confusing thoughts will likely keep you awake at night as they replay in your head. You might begin to question your mortality and the mortality of those you care about. Each day, you yearn for the one you lost, wishing that they could somehow be brought back to you. Even if you know that this isn't possible, you still put a lot of time and energy into thinking about this.

This stage, which is often accompanied by anxiety and anger, can feel consuming. Throughout this time, you are likely to feel tired and lethargic, and your daily routines are probably more difficult than before. Doing the bare minimum here is usually all that you are capable of. You have just lost a loved one, so do not be too hard on yourself. If you can only do a little bit, celebrate your small accomplishments. Forgive yourself for not being able to operate at 100% like you used to. This is the point of mourning; it is a period where you shift your focus to fully accept the loss of your loved one.

You will likely do a lot of internalized thinking. Even if you cannot share these thoughts with other people yet, you will think deeply about searching for meaning. Whether you are thinking about the meaning of life as a whole or the meaning behind why your loved one was taken from you, this becomes a point where you are likely to appear outwardly pensive. If others ask you if you need anything or if you are okay, remember that they have good intentions. You might still be resistant to help, but make sure that you can see that you still have good people in your life who want the best for you.

Disorganization and Despair: Once you move into this phase, you will feel an abundance of emotions. This can feel especially intense if you were closed-off in stage one. Once you begin to accept the reality of the loss, all of the feelings that were formulating in your brain are going to rise to the surface. They may surprise you as you cycle through various ones each day. One day, you might wake up feeling sad and down. The next, you might feel angry at those around you. Because of this, the most realistic solution for you might be to withdraw from others in your life. Whether you don't want to hurt them or feel that you cannot interact with them, you are at risk of isolating yourself.

Withdrawal often begins during this stage. If you usually have hobbies and habits that keep you happy or entertained, you might notice yourself stepping away from them. While it is ideal to keep yourself occupied in positive ways that will promote positive coping mechanisms, it isn't always easy to continue your life the way that it was before you lost your loved one. Every little thing is likely going to start reminding you of this person, and this can make routines difficult.

It isn't uncommon to seek a change during this phase of grief. You might want to take up a new hobby, spend time around different people, or even change something about your physical appearance. Anything that separates your sadness of the loss from the person you are now will help you cope.

It is especially important in this stage to pay close attention to the way you are coping. If you are using your coping mechanisms as crutches or excuses not to take care of your responsibilities, this is a sign that you have become too withdrawn. There must be a balance within every phase if you want to move through it successfully. The goal is to reach acceptance, and you can only do this if you have the drive to get through the point that you are currently in. While you may feel stuck and hopeless, there are always ways to pull yourself back up. Use the resources you have around you. If someone reaches out to you, try to respond to them. It will benefit you in the long run, even if it initially pushes you out of your comfort zone.

Reorganization and Recovery: At this point, you recognize that your life is forever changed. You can see that there will be permanent differences in your life now that your loved one has passed away, but you are more accepting of them than you used to be. Some days will still be exceptionally difficult, but you have more strength to get through these bad moments. You understand now that this is your new version of normal, and you might have thoughts about what you can do in your daily life to honor your loved one who has passed on.

Wanting your loved one to be proud of you is a common feeling after you have mourned. This is a point in your life where you might want to change your habits or behaviors to become a better person. In this way, the loss can make you more motivated and productive. It gives you a new perspective to consider about life and what you are doing in it. This point is not an easy one to reach, but it is a worthwhile journey that ends up bringing positivity into your life.

The energy that you feel you lost during the beginning stages of mourning will be renewed. All of the activities and things that you used to love before will start to bring you joy once again. Slowly but surely, your life will feel secure again, and you will reach a point where you can fondly remember your loved one. However, this does not mean you have stopped grieving. You can reach this point yet feel like you still need more time to grieve, and that is okay. Going forward, each moment is going to become easier for you.

Though Parkes's stages of grief are clearly outlined and recognized by many people worldwide, it is still not a universal model that works on everybody who has lost a loved one. Grief is complex in the way that it affects people, and some doctors do not believe that this model applies to grieving individuals because they reject the idea it exists. Due to inconclusive evidence, some psychiatrists completely reject both Parkes's model and Kübler-Ross's model. For example, Russell P. Friedman, executive director of the Grief Recovery Institute, claims that no study accurately showcases the positive evidence that surrounds the idea of grieving (Shermer 2008). He believes that grief is natural and cannot be charted with bullet points and milestones.

Robert A. Neimeyer, a University of Memphis psychologist, feels the same way about the subject. He wrote a book, *Meaning Reconstruction and the Experience of Loss*, which describes grief as a process that has no clear point of "recovery." Despite some studies, he does not see any viable evidence that suggests grief can be charted in a way that would indicate which stage you are on and how far away you are from said point of recovery. While there are many different opinions on the matter, it helps to hear both sides of the topic. Since grief is an entirely personal experience, you might find that the models help you cope with the loss. If they do not, however, there is no need to fret since they are not universal or guaranteed.

While many different theories and models have been formed to describe the process of grieving, there is one commonality; it happens in stages. No matter which model you believe in, you are going to have to work through your own experiences to determine what makes you feel better and what will allow you to move on to the next stage.

4

FINDING SOLACE IN STOICISM

There is a branch of philosophy called Stoicism that can help you find solace within your grieving period. Through the Stoic principles, you will be able to feel happier, more resilient, and wiser. This philosophy has helped me conquer many obstacles in my life and the wisdom is timeless and relevant even to this day.

Beginning around 340 BC in ancient Greece, Stoicism is a philosophy that is still widely recognized and used. It focuses on how to handle hardship while maintaining a strong exterior. Stoics are often known as being emotionless, but they are simply trained to process their emotions right away rather than letting them linger.

The founding of Stoicism began with a merchant named Zeno, who was shipwrecked as he was traveling to Athens and lost everything on board. The wealthy merchant continued to Athens, where he visited a bookstore and read a book that introduced him to the work of Socrates. He was so inspired by what he read that he sought out other philosophers and became acquainted with the Cynic philosopher Crates and the Megarian philosopher Stiplo. They taught Zeno about philosophy, which changed his life and his outlook on the negative events in his life. He began to see his ship-wreck as a magnificent voyage because he was introduced to these viewpoints.

Settling in Stoa Poikile, which translates to "painted porch," Zeno began teaching and leading philosophical discussions. Originally, his followers were called Zenoians, but they eventually became known as Stoics. Zeno went on to found a school that taught people about Stoicism and its principles, including that:

- Nature is always rational.
- The universe operates based on the law of reason, and humans cannot escape its force.
- To live a virtuous life, you must be rational.
- Wisdom is the key virtue you must strive for; the other cardinal virtues stem from wisdom, and they are insight, bravery, justice, and self-control.
- Poverty, death, and illness are not inherently evil.
- You should feel a dutiful reason to seek virtue, not a pleasurable reason.

Nearly every other religious or spiritual school that came before his school was named after its creator, but Zeno's school was an excep-tion. His new way of thinking spread, and many great Stoic philoso-phers followed him. Marcus Aurelius, Seneca, and Epictetus are among some of the most famous, and their works and wisdom are still referenced to this day.

THE STOICS

MARCUS AURELIUS

Roman emperor Marcus Aurelius was born in 121 AD. By the time Marcus Aurelius reached his teenage years, the current emperor, Hadrian, was childless and close to reaching his death. Hadrian's first choice as a successor had died unexpectedly, so he was made to choose another—Antoninus, the uncle of Marcus Aurelius. Antoninus adopted Marcus Aurelius, and once Hadrian passed away, Marcus Aurelius was next in line to become emperor after Antoninus.

Marcus Aurelius became emperor in 161 AD, and his rule of the Roman Empire lasted for nearly two decades, up until his death in 180 AD. Throughout his reign, he relied on Stoicism to guide him as a leader, particularly during his military campaigns.

During the years of military conflict, Marcus Aurelius wrote himself private notes that centered around Stoicism. These became the backbone of his famous work, *Meditations*, which is one of the best sources of the principles of Stoicism. These private writings helped Marcus Aurelius to pick himself back up during the rough years of conflict, and they are evidence of his inner strength and the virtues that guided him.

Some of the main lessons we can learn today from Marcus Aurelius include:

Practice Virtues You Can Show

If you feel that you lack certain abilities or skills, it is easy to fall into a pit of self-doubt. During this process of losing faith in yourself, you also lose the ability to realize the things that you are amazing at. To combat this feeling, focus on the things that come naturally to you, what you are already good at. This becomes your foundation for any future self-esteem you develop. If you cannot think of anything that you excel at, take the time to write down each skill that you have. No matter how small or insignificant, write it down, and you might see that you are capable of so much more than you realize. It is quick and easy to list off all of the things you cannot do, but when was the last time you told someone about all of the things you can do?

Draw Strength From Others

Marcus Aurelius was no stranger to seeking inspiration from other people in his life. He had teachers and mentors who influenced him throughout his lifetime, and without their influence, he probably would not have grown to become the wonderful Stoic that he was. To gain strength from others, you must be open to the idea that you cannot possibly know everything. Even after a lifetime of studying, observing, and learning, there is always more to discover. Other people have different life experiences from you, and having conversations with them while keeping an open mind will allow you to expand upon your ideas. Allowing new perspectives is how you can draw strength from those you admire most. Having many role models is common for those who follow Stoic principles.

Focus on the Present

Knowing that temptations exist all around us, Marcus Aurelius was a firm believer in controlling your mind. It is easy to use your imagination to think about what the worst outcome of any given situation is, but you can also use it in a way that will help you progress in life. By focusing on the present and what you can control, you will feel more prepared for your future. Many people start to panic at the thought of the future because they are too worried about the factors that might begin to work against them. Your imagination can become a big tool that you can use, but make sure that you are using it in the right way, a way that uplifts you. Crippling fear will paralyze you if you let it.

SENECA

A Roman philosopher and statesman, Seneca became an influential Stoic in the mid-1st century AD. He was born into a wealthy family, and he came from a lineage of other influential people. As a young boy, Seneca was brought to Rome by his aunt. There, he studied to be an orator and learned philosophy. The school he attended was the School of Sextii, which combined Stoicism and Neo-Pythagoreanism. On a great track in life, it seemed like Seneca had a wonderful future ahead.

One of Seneca's first hardships was the decline of his health. To recover, he moved to Egypt where his aunt and her family cared for him. Once he was healed, he made his way back to Rome in the year

31. It was then that he switched paths, starting a career in politics and law. Fairly quickly, he grew to severely dislike the emperor, Caligula, because of their opposing views. They were on such bad terms that at one point, the emperor ordered Seneca to commit suicide, although he later agreed to spare Seneca's life because he stated that it would be a short one.

In the year 41, Seneca was accused of adultery with the emperor's niece. Claudius, the emperor at the time, banished Seneca to Corsica. During this time, Seneca did not succumb to his punishment. Instead, he thrived and wrote *Consolations*. Eventually, he was allowed back to Rome in the year 49 thanks to the emperor's wife's persuasion. He became a praetor, part of the Roman magistrate, and became tutor to the future emperor Nero.

In the year 54, Claudius was murdered, and Nero became emperor. As Nero's tutor, Seneca's importance grew, and he was even responsible for writing Nero's first speech. Despite his success, Seneca was continually accused of various plots by his political enemies. Unlike a lot of politicians at the time, Seneca had a more humane attitude toward slaves, and he aimed for more fiscal and judicial reform. Many did not agree with this, so he quickly became hated.

Eventually, Seneca fell out of favor, and he died in the year 65. Stoicism continued to spread, and Seneca's memory was kept alive through the teachings of the Stoic leaders who came after him. By the time the 16th century arrived, Senecan style prose had become prominent. People who wrote literature, essays, and sermons often used Senecan style to convey their important messages.

212 | LIVING WITH LOSS

Seneca held several beliefs that are still relevant today, including:

Find an Anchor

Seneca was a believer in seeking inspiration from outside sources, who could serve as anchors in life. To find your anchor, you must find a role model. This person is someone who will influence you. When you do not know what decision to make, think about this person and what they might do. Through their principles, it is thought that we can get one step closer to living a good life, a Stoic goal.

Never Be a Slave of Your Wealth

Though Seneca did come from wealth, he did not simply ride on the coattails of his family. He worked hard to get where he was in his political career, and he continued to work hard on his writing until the day he was forced to death. Seneca was always one to ensure that he was not being too influenced by his privilege, which is a great philosophy to keep in mind, even today.

Fight Your Ego

Seneca had a great deal of confidence and self-esteem, but he did not allow this to go to his head. It is important to make sure that we remain humble. Seneca warned others to never give in to indulgence as this would be a certain downfall to the ego.

EPICTETUS

Unlike the other Stoic influences we have covered above, Epictetus was born a slave, proving that Stoicism can be useful to anyone in any stage of life. Though Epictetus had a different upbringing and more hardship than most, he was still able to use Stoic principles to help guide him along the way.

He was born almost 2,000 years ago in present-day Turkey. His owner, Epaphroditus, allowed him to pursue the study of liberal arts, enabling him to learn about a subject that he was passionate about—philosophy. The Stoic Musonius Rufus became his mentor, and his influence guided Epictetus in many ways.

After emperor Nero's death, Epictetus gained his freedom. He then went on to teach philosophy in Rome for over two decades. This path lasted until Domitian became the emperor and banished all Roman philosophers. Not allowing this to stop him, Epictetus fled to Greece where he went on to found his school of philosophy. He put all of his efforts into this school and teaching until the day he died, a prime example of how he did not allow the hardship in his life to overtake his accomplishments and dreams. Even with his upbringing as a slave, Epictetus never gave up on what he was passionate about.

Another difference between Epictetus and other influential Stoics is that Epictetus never drafted any of his work or chose to publish his beliefs. By an amazing stroke of luck, his influence as a teacher lived on through the notes that were taken by his students. These notes show us that Epictetus seemed to always unintentionally take a different path than most. One big lesson learned from this is that you cannot always choose what happens to you, but you can choose to make the most of it. Instead of wasting your time and energy worrying about the things that are already happening, you can take a more productive route.

As always, there are lessons to be learned from this notable Stoic:

Remember What You Have Control Of

This is one of the biggest Stoic principles to remember. Epictetus had nearly every challenge in his life to deter him, but he never allowed this to set him back. He still went on to pursue his dreams because he chose to focus on the elements he had control of.

Some things are simply going to be outside of our control. No matter how much we prepare for certain things to happen, there are still outside factors that can influence the final result. We might believe that we are ready for any of these options, only to be surprised when the situation takes a turn. This is enough to upset or overwhelm the average person, but Stoics train to work with any result that they are met with.

You can only focus on yourself in any situation. Once you have taken all of the necessary precautions, you must use the energy you have left to work on what you can do to improve your life. Think about what you can do to change anything unfavorable, and do not give up because you think that there is nothing more that can be done. There is always more if you look for it.

Set the Standard

Stoicism teaches us that we must be brave when it comes to being open to change. Epictetus did not believe in lecturing people by using persuasion. Instead, he wanted to be a living example of the principles he believed in. He thought that would make a much more convincing argument.

You need to let your actions speak loud and clear. If you have beliefs, you must act in accordance with them at all times. This gives you credibility among those around you. Instead of convincing others to stand by your side, you must set a standard of being that will convince them on their own.

If you are looking for a role model and evaluating different people, consider what put them in this ideal position. It was likely their actions that drew you in. They convinced you to listen to what they had to say and why their viewpoints mattered.

Life is all about the choices you make. If you are unhappy with the choices you have made so far, you can always make changes. You can completely transform your life if you are willing to try something different.

Create Your Character

Habits have a big influence on nearly all humans. Epictetus was aware of this, and he always encouraged his students to break free from the norm.

When we rely on habits too much, we become oblivious to other opportunities that we encounter. Imagine that you are used to driving to work the same way every day. There are other ways you can drive, maybe some that will save you time by avoiding traffic, but you have always used the same route. This is an example of a way that your habits and routines might be holding you back. They are keeping you in a stagnant state of being that makes it more difficult to branch out.

Many things in life define your character, and all of them come together to create who you are as a person. It is not easy to make changes in routines and habits because these are things that keep you feeling secure. They allow you to feel that you are accomplished and safe. Sometimes, though, it is necessary to rattle this feeling of security without fully breaking your spirit. Show yourself that there are other steps you can take to achieve the same results. If you open your mind to these new ways, you might be surprised at what you find.

STOICISM IN MODERN TIMES

While learning about the ancient practice of Stoic philosophy can be interesting, you might be wondering how these principles apply to the world we live in today. You can take some inspiration from Ultimate Fighting Championship (UFC) champion Khabib Nurmagomedov. In less than two rounds in October 2020, he was able to choke out his opponent. This secured his lightweight championship belt. As soon as the fight came to its conclusion, Nurmagomedov collapsed to the ground in tears. This is an unusual sight for a UFC fighter, especially since they are known for their grit and tough demeanor. Later that day, he announced his retirement. Considering that he was ending on a high note, it is easy to see how this could have contributed to his stream of emotions.

On a deeper level, Nurmagomedov was also going through the grieving process. Just three months before the fight, he lost his father. This fight that he had just dominated was the first that he had ever fought without his dad there in his corner. His mom wanted him to stop fighting after this, and he agreed that it would be for the best.

Nurmagomedov did not want to continue now that his father was gone. It was a difficult and bittersweet moment for him as he wept on the floor and later announced his retirement, but he proved his strength and tenacity by giving an impressive battle.

Stoicism often allows people to look strong and powerful on the outside. If you just looked at Nurmagomedov in the octagon, you would have never guessed that he was going through a recent loss. He took all of his courage and focus and channeled it into his fight, and it paid off. After the relief he felt once he won the fight that only he knew was going to be his final one, he was able to release all of the emotions that were being kept inside.

His Stoic approach to managing his emotions got him through all of the suffering he had to endure. Because of the loss of his father, he was placed in a position to either forfeit his fight or to continue. He decided to channel his strength to continue, and it showed him exactly what he was capable of. You will encounter many moments in your life that will ask you to stand strong in the face of adversity. While you might not be fighting in the UFC, you will have to put on that bravery to get you through the moment just like Nurmagomedov did.

STOICISM: DEATH AND GRIEF

The Stoics had a lot to say about death and grief because they are so natural and such a big part of the human experience. Many classic Stoic texts feature the topic of death because it is one of the things most outside of our control. After all, every human has a life that they can choose to live to their fullest, but they typically do not know when it is going to end. This can feel like a daunting thought to many people, especially as they begin to experience the loss of loved ones in their lives. You do not want to live a life that is tethered to the fear of death or dying. Instead, you can take a page from the Stoics' book and learn how to view death as intended—a natural phenomenon.

The Stoics were well known for remembering their mortality. They even had the phrase "memento mori," which translates to "remember death." The Stoics did not want to think about death in a fearful or impending doom type of way. Instead, they aimed to become aware of their mortality and how things could change in an instant. They knew that no matter how successful they were or how well-versed they were in life, they were still going to meet the same fate as every other human on the planet. This can become a comforting thought if you allow it to.

With memento mori as a tool for guidance, the Stoics did not forget about how limited their time on Earth was. Whenever they needed extra motivation to persevere, they considered that their time was not infinite. They needed to pursue their passions sooner rather than later or else they might miss out on the opportunity to do so at all.

Epictetus took this one step further with a somewhat controversial reminder that he told others to keep in mind. He advised people to think about tucking their children into bed at night. Then, he told them to imagine what it would be like if their children were no longer there. Waking up without them would be devastating, and the thought further proves that the Stoic principle of being present in the moment is so important.

Using an "ignorance is bliss" approach was never recommended by the Stoics. While this does keep you free of the fear that can come attached to the idea of death, it leaves you feeling too unprepared when it happens. The shock of this moment can debilitate you if you ignore it until it is happening to you. Open your eyes to the death that surrounds you in your life already. Turn to nature; even the simplest of plants and trees die. This is going to desensitize you to death, in a way.

While there is nothing that can ever truly prepare you for the loss of a loved one, a general acceptance of the nature of death is helpful.

Conquering the Fear

It is within the Stoic belief that we should conquer death by learning how to use it productively. To do so, we must learn how to see it objectively.

Seneca wrote a letter of condolence to his mother, and in this letter, he acknowledged that the rule of Fortune is harsh and unfavorable. He also reminded her that it is now in her control to either endure the suffering or succumb to it. While it cannot always be avoided and while it is not always deserved, we must learn how to power through it to become strong enough to move into the next stage of grief.

A question posed to the Stoics is how to make sense of this harsh reality that can often feel cruel. How does one come to terms with the fact that we are eventually going to lose a lot of people we love and that there is nothing we can do to stop it?

One thing we can do is to stop catastrophizing the concept. Death is terrible and sad, but it does not have to be a looming presence in our lives at all times. When we are not mourning, we must be living. Other things are going to happen in our lives that are going to allow us to feel emotions.

A common misconception about Stoicism that affects grieving is that Stoics do not like to tap into their emotions, that they want people to suppress them. This is not true, though.

The Stoic philosophy teaches us to face our emotions head-on. When we experience a loss or have to deal with death, it is thought that we should begin processing the emotions as soon as possible. This will allow them to pass so they no longer hinder us in life. Running from your emotions only provides you with temporary relief. It all goes back to the "ignorance is bliss" mentality. All of the emotions that you run from will eventually catch up with you. Then, you will have to face them, and you might feel even less prepared to do so.

If you tell other people in your life that you are fine and insist you do not need to talk about your emotions, you are suppressing your feelings. This hinders your healing process and makes you feel like you are being overpowered by the difficult feelings you are struggling with.

Many people seek distractions to get their mind off of the loss, but this can work both to your advantage and disadvantage. Stoicism warns against too much distraction, but a little can prove to be helpful. When you find healthy coping mechanisms that can help to make you feel like yourself again, you will be better able to process the emotions that you are left with.

Face the pain now. If you are going to take one lesson from the Stoics regarding grief, this should be it. Take away any expectations that you have about the process because, much like death, it is not going to be predictable. See where your feelings take you, and understand that it isn't always going to be a smooth ride. It will get easier, though. The more that you process your feelings, the more strength you will obtain. Rely on your inner strength to conquer your grief while remembering that this is a natural part of your life.

More Advice

Seneca urged people to speak with their friends and family members to fondly remember the person who passed away. Through memories shared, this person is kept alive in a way.

But this can be difficult because many people who know you are going through a difficult loss might be unsure of how to approach you. They will be cautious of upsetting you, but if you make it clear that you are willing to talk about fond memories of the person who has died, they will be better able to help you get through this difficult time. Having others to talk to about the person you have lost will provide you with a nice sense of solidarity that counteracts the loneliness you may also feel.

Marcus Aurelius gave some advice in his *Meditations*. He explained that you can be grateful for those important people in your life before they pass away. He started his book with a list of the people relevant to his life, and he urged others to do the same. Before any loss happens, or if it has already occurred, you can make a list of everyone in your life you currently feel grateful for. These individuals can bring you many different positive traits, which help you to live and behave at your best. They also allow you to be your true self because a level of trust is formed that just is not present when you are surrounded by people you do not know well or people who do not have your best intentions at heart.

Thinking about the ancient Stoic times, you can rest assured that these people also dealt with the struggles that come with death and the hardship that comes with grieving. You are not alone in this journey, no matter how much it feels this way. Dealing with death and loss is a part of being a human being, and you can gain inspiration from all of these Stoic individuals who have gone through it before. Harness their strength to get you through your journey.

Negative Visualization

One way that all three of the above Stoic philosophers worked through hard times is by practicing the art of negative visualization. This is a type of visualization that allows you to predict worst-case scenarios before they happen to you. To do this, you must foresee the bad things that could potentially come your way. It takes self-control to do this, of course, because it is easy to overthink the possibilities. The result is going to be more favorable because you will either be better prepared for the bad event or it will not occur.

If this sounds like the opposite of positive thinking, that's because it is. Negative visualization goes against everything that positive thinking stands for. This can be taken as a pessimistic outlook on life to some onlookers, but true Stoicism is not pessimistic. It is a matter of hoping for the best yet preparing for the worst. The Stoics were not frequently faced with disappointment thanks to the art of negative visualization. Because they were always mindful of the potential negative events to come, they were not often caught off guard if they happened.

When you find yourself scared of a specific situation, for example, the loss of a loved one, try negative visualization. You know that death is natural, and it will occur. However, you might not know if you will lose your loved one first or if they will lose you first. Naturally, the thought is unsettling. You can imagine each possibility to better prepare yourself for any outcome. When my mom knew her time was coming to an end, she always told my brother and I we needed to take care of her dog. Although, this thought pained me as our family dog was most attached to her, in a way it helped me imagine my life without her. It was the last thing I wanted, but at this point it was inevitable. It made me think of how I would take care of the dog, talking it on walks and feeding her. This visualization made me a lot less scared and anxious of the future. Although this practice is not ideal, there is some power behind it.

Remember, though, that Stoicism is rational and logical. Do not get too carried away with the negative thoughts, but allow them to guide you to each conclusion. It is like exploring the "what ifs" that always pop into your head. Some might argue that you should simply ignore those thoughts, but addressing them directly can be enough to put them at ease and to remove the fear.

There are several ways you can go about negative visualization if you'd like to try it out in your life. You can picture your daily routine and all of the inconveniences that might occur during it. Think about how you would handle getting caught up in traffic or dealing with difficult clients at work. Maybe you burn dinner and get into an argument with your spouse. Anything can happen, and even if it seems minor, it is still going to impact you.

The other way you can go about negative visualization is to directly imagine the loss that you fear. Think about it head-on, and pay attention to the emotions that this brings forth.

It does take practice to master the art of negative visualization. One positive part of facing depression or depressive symptoms is that it can allow you to better practice this art. Since you are naturally going to be imagining the worst things you can think of, explore these feelings and how to better get ahold of them. You do not need to be brought further down by the thoughts that live in your head; you can rise above them while still paying close attention.

Writings on Death and Grief

While Stoicism lives on today through those who practice it, they learn what they know from the ancient texts written by the great leaders who have passed away. Through reading the writings in this section, you might be able to discover a new outlook on death that does not scare you or impact you in the same way as it used to.

Seneca's *Dialogues and Letters* provides you with a letter that he wrote to console his mother. Her mother died while giving birth to her, which naturally impacted her deeply. His mother was also dealt an unfortunate blow when she found out that her grandson passed away. This happened only days before Seneca was banished from Rome. This specific story is called *Consolation to Helvia.* Seneca shares his musings on grief in this letter, and there is much to learn from it.

While Epictetus did not write in the same way that Seneca did, his teachings have still been compiled into a work called *The Discourses.* Here, you can find his sentiments on the mortality of the ones we love. He guides us through thoughts about the idea of loss, which can prove helpful when we are forced to suddenly let go. Instead of thinking about the loss as a devastating tragedy, Epictetus preferred to think of it as a "sweet sadness" in your heart. This stems from the idea that you can still remember your loved ones fondly, especially after they pass. Their memories will remain alive in your heart.

Of course, Marcus Aurelius' work titled *Meditations* has been referenced several times in this book. It remains a prominent collection of writing that not only explains Stoicism in a great way but also helps you to work through your grief. He talks a lot about life and death and how they relate to one another. When you think about death as a part of a cycle rather than a standalone event, you can broaden your mind to the idea that it is a natural part of life. He provides his readers with great advice on how to get the best start to each of your days and how to live with a sense of honor in everything that you do.

It may seem intimidating to read about grief, especially if you are currently in the thick of it, but each of these writings has a lot to offer, and they are worth exploring.

5

FACE YOUR PAIN AND YOUR GRIEF

To face the pain you feel from the loss you have endured, you must start at the first step—handling your avoidance. There are two different types of avoidance that people typically go through when they discover they have lost a loved one. Some avoid participating in activities that remind them of their loved ones. The memories that arise might be too painful to face because a lot of them are going to be centered around the person who is gone. The second type of avoidance is when you avoid something that once made you happy or will make you happy. There is a sense of guilt that can arise when you are dealing with a loss. The voice in the back of your head might be telling you that you do not deserve to be happy because your loved one has passed away.

There is a third way that grief might be avoided, and it is more subtle. Some people opt for distractions that will keep them busy. This might not seem problematic on the outside, but it is still a method that allows you to avoid thinking about the sadness and pain that you are feeling. This can look like taking on extra shifts at work or immersing yourself in a hobby that prevents you from having too much free time. You might subconsciously begin to stay busy because your brain knows that stillness will bring forth the dark thoughts.

HOW DO YOU KNOW IF YOU ARE BEING AVOIDANT?

You must learn the difference between a healthy distraction and avoidance because the line is subtle. When you are grieving, you are more likely to make decisions outside of your character. This happens because you feel so uncomfortable due to all of the sadness.

Pay attention to the choices that you make during this time. They are going to be telling of how well you are working through your grief. If you notice that you are changing your routines and habits, question yourself. Think about whether or not the things you are filling your time with are helping you and making you happy or simply keeping you occupied so you do not feel overwhelmed. There are moments when the process is going to feel impossible, but you will still be able to find a healthy distraction to get you through it.

For a distraction to be healthy, you must be participating in an activity that lessens the intensity of your sadness and pain. You are not supposed to completely do away with your pain because that is not realistic, but anything healthy for you will help you have a moment to breathe. When using a distraction, be sure to give yourself breaks from time to time so that you can check in with yourself frequently.

The main focus of your healthy distractions should always be your well-being. Ask yourself if what you are doing is benefitting you. If so, in what ways? Identifying this will make it easier for you to determine if you are engaging in a healthy distraction or not.

When you take a little break from your grief, remember that it is only temporary. You will return to it later. The break is not your result but a moment for you to recollect your thoughts. This will lessen the intensity of all of the bad feelings, especially on your hard days.

All of your days might feel like hard days when you first lose someone you love, but this is okay. You can engage in a healthy distraction daily if it helps you. As time goes on, you will find the need to rely on this distraction less and less. Still, you are learning a healthy management technique for your emotions. Activities that allow you to feel rejuvenated will greatly benefit your well-being. Some examples include:

- Breathing exercises
- Yoga
- Meditation
- Massage
- Reading
- Relaxing

Your healthy distraction should also be deliberate; it is something you do by choice and with control. Avoidance techniques are often chosen outside of your control. You might find yourself doing certain things that you do not remember deciding on. This is a key difference between the two actions. Every time you are engaging in a healthy distraction, you should feel positive about it because you chose it for yourself.

The activities that you find healing might differ from those that others find healing. You need to listen to your mind and body to discover which ones are personally restorative to you. Make sure whatever you do does not just provide short-term gratification.

Some activities that you might engage in will only provide you with the feeling of instant gratification. You will feel better at first, but then, your condition will worsen. Shopping to fill a void is an example of one of these behaviors. It might feel great to spend money because it is distracting, but this isn't necessarily restorative to your mental health.

Be wary of the way that you use your healthy coping behaviors as well. While watching your favorite movie can be incredibly healing, watching it late at night and disrupting your sleep pattern can cause you to feel tired at work. You need to keep in mind that there are limits that come along with every behavior, even the healthy ones. Be smart about the way you are caring for yourself and treating yourself. This will directly impact your ability to get through your grief.

Most people imagine relaxing activities when they think about healthy coping mechanisms, but this does not always have to be the case. You can engage your mind in healthy ways, too. Using your creativity during this time can be a great way to get your feelings out. You can paint, draw, write, sing, and act to engage that inner creativity. Exercise is another form of healthy behavior. This one works especially well because it provides you with endorphins simultaneously. These are the happy chemicals that uplift your mood. Experiment with some of these things as a way of including them in your routine again.

If you are still having trouble deciding if an activity is healthy, ask yourself if it is practical. If you find something that you love and that makes you feel great, it is not going to do any good if it drains you of your resources. For example, you might enjoy going out to sing karaoke with friends. This can be a fun thing to do every once in a while, but going every other day is going to drain you of your money and energy. You must still practice self-control, even through grief. Giving in to all of your desires will not help you heal; it will only create more problems for you to fix in the long run.

The last thing you need is to pick up on some bad habits during your grieving process. They are more likely to become permanent fixtures in your life because you are relying on them more heavily than you normally would. While it is hard, you still need to consider your future. Do not make decisions in your life without considering how they will affect you right now and in the future. You can allow yourself to give in to your guilty pleasures sometimes, but you should also know that this isn't going to become a regular habit.

Your healthy distractions will often involve other people. Spending time around other people is a fast and effective way to get your mind off of anything draining. The energy that they bring into your life can help you a lot, and this is why you must make sure you are only surrounding yourself with the best people. Be sure that the people you allow to get close to you have your best intentions in mind. They will want you to be happy, and they should be willing to engage in healthy coping behaviors with you so you do not feel alone. If someone begins to influence you to pick up on bad habits, then this person likely does not have your best intentions in mind. They might mean well, but you need to stand up for yourself and know what is right.

Management Strategies

Now that you are aware of the difference between avoidant behaviors and healthy coping behaviors, you can learn how to help yourself when you are feeling your worst. Remember that avoidant behavior takes more effort than healthy behavior. You will likely spend twice as long thinking about how to avoid unpleasant emotions instead of simply confronting them. Understandably, you are not always going to be able to confront them right away, and that is okay. This is why you should give yourself breaks where you can engage in healthy behaviors.

A pattern that will help you spot avoidant behaviors follows:

Stressful trigger > negative thought and physical response > feeling overwhelmed > avoid activity or thoughts that involve the trigger

When you notice that this is taking place, pause for a second. Take a few deep breaths, then ask yourself these questions:

- What am I trying to avoid?
- What has my current coping mechanism(s) cost me?
- How much time do I spend on avoidance?
- Am I being avoidant due to fear of something or someone?

Next, you need to reflect on your answers. To find a balance, think about a healthy distraction that is short and easy for you to engage in. This should be something that does not deplete you or your resources. While being mindful of the activities you choose, you will notice an improvement in the avoidance pattern that you used to follow.

As you think about the activities you'd like to incorporate into your routine, ask yourself if each one reduces the negativity you are experiencing in your life. See if it makes your hardship easier to manage. If the answer is no, then you should probably move on to the next activity.

You might also be able to come up with a creative resolution that allows you to engage in the activity without straining yourself. For example, again, imagine that going to the karaoke bar with your friends brings you joy. Since this is something you cannot do every day, you might take up singing at home for a few minutes each day. While this is not the same experience, it might be a step in the right direction.

You also need to allow yourself some time to think about solutions. It isn't common to know right away which activities will help you heal. It might take several weeks or even months to come up with anything at all. Do not feel discouraged, and always remain open to suggestions. The people in your life might share advice with you based on what is working for them or what they have done in the past. Since you do not have to go with their suggestion automatically, there is no pressure to act. Simply listen to what they have to say. If this is someone who cares about you, they are likely telling you because they do not want to see you suffering.

Why Avoidance Won't Work

Sadness is not a feeling your brain wants to experience, so it will naturally do everything it can to avoid it. Your mind might choose to focus on ideas that are not relevant to you just so it does not have to feel these unpleasant emotions such as sadness. Most would argue that part of the meaning of life is to find true happiness. This can feel difficult after you have lost a loved one. Since your life now feels different, maybe dark, it is harder to figure out which path you need to take to get to happiness. When you become a prisoner of your dark thoughts, the avoidance comes quickly. Your brain will desperately try to grasp at this method until you can feel a fraction of relief.

It is going to be difficult to break free from this pattern, but you are capable of doing it. You can change your life, even as you are grieving. To do that, though, you must recognize the patterns of avoidance you are relying on. The following are some examples of avoidance and why they do not work. Use them to inspire you to make changes. Seek strength in knowing that there are other ways you can make yourself feel better during this time.

Work or Daily Tasks

The thing about grief is that it is not patient. It will not politely step aside as you go to work and complete your daily tasks. Often, tending to your responsibilities while you are grieving can trigger a lot of avoidance. These tasks are going to feel much harder than they usually do and might prove to be a struggle. On the other hand, you might feel the need to immerse yourself in your work. By taking on extra shifts and more hours, you might believe you are productively handling your grief. As you already know, this is not balanced, and balance is necessary to find a better way to cope with your grief.

If you stop completing your tasks, you are going to be met with a lot of stress. This happens because you have too much free time to focus on your sadness and pain. As the deadlines begin to catch up with you, it will feel incredibly overwhelming. If you choose to over-work yourself, you will not have a free moment to think. While this might feel better than thinking too much, it is still avoidance to a high degree. As you know, there needs to be time set aside for you to ponder the way you feel. The emotions need to be addressed if you want them to pass.

Caring for Others

Caring for other people instead of yourself during a period of grief is common, especially if the person who has passed away left behind a spouse or other family member. It might feel good to do this good deed, but the activity can become immersive and draining in itself. Taking on a caregiver role feels natural to many, and this can be a kind gesture, but you must ensure that you are still keeping your life balanced.

Set boundaries with your emotions. If you feel that you have nothing left to give to other people, then you definitely won't have anything left for yourself. You must always save some time and energy to spend on yourself and your well-being, even if you can only manage one form of self-care. Anything that you were not doing before is going to feel like an improvement.

Drugs or Alcohol

Unfortunately, many people find it easy to abuse substances while they are grieving. This happens because these substances are highly addictive. When mixed with sadness and an addictive personality, the result is not going to be good. If you notice that you are becoming reliant on substances, seek help immediately.

Seeking treatment during this time can be a blessing in disguise. Not only will you be able to work through the substance abuse problem, but you can also learn how to sort through your feelings surrounding the loss. Try to let your guard down if this is the case. It might feel shameful, but getting help is a lot better than letting the problem persist and worsen.

Travel

Traveling can be great when you are feeling stuck in a phase of your life. Getting out of the same environment that you are always in will feel refreshing, but remember your balance; you cannot travel forever. If you find yourself going on back-to-back trips, you might need to slow down and check in with your emotions.

Use travel sparingly as a coping mechanism because it can be a form of escapism. For example, going on a weekend drive into the next town can serve as a great way to promote healing. You can experience a different atmosphere temporarily. When you return to your environment, you should feel rejuvenated and ready to take on your healing process once again.

Isolating

Isolating yourself while you are grieving can come naturally. Since you do not feel like yourself, you might not want to subject other people in your life to this energy. In a way, you will feel like you are doing other people a favor because you do not want to feel like a burden. Taking a little alone time can be a healthy way to sit with your thoughts and address them, but remain mindful of how much time you are taking.

While you don't need to jump straight back into socialization, you should make an effort to see some people in your life who you love. Do not commit to long or complex plans. Sitting down with a friend over coffee to talk can be an easy way to transition into talking to other people. Be easy on yourself, and take your time.

COMMON PATTERNS FOR GRIEF AVOIDANCE

We looked at one avoidance pattern in the previous section, but there are several more to be aware of. These avoidance patterns tend to appear after you lose a loved one, and you will probably be able to identify with one or more of them in the beginning. By paying close attention to them, you will be able to stop any unhealthy behavioral patterns before they enter your daily routine.

The Procrastinator

This type of avoidance revolves around the idea that if you ignore your pain for long enough, the grieving period will pass on its own. While it might feel this way with avoidance, you already know that this is not true. The period of grief isn't passing when you "procrastinate" your mourning. It might go away for a while as long as you can keep up with the distractions, but it will return to you when you least expect it.

Grief and sadness are easily triggered. One day, you might see something that reminds you of the person you lost, and all of your memories of that person will come flooding back. This will eventually lead you to the conclusion that they are gone, and you will likely spiral into a wave of depression and dark thoughts. It is an overwhelming burden to take on all at once.

The procrastinator type might believe that giving in to grief is a sign of weakness. Instead of crying and thinking about their emotions, the person might believe that it is better to toughen up. This means that walls are being put up in an attempt to stifle the emotions that are trying to surface. It might seem like this person is incredibly strong, but this is only the case until they are triggered into experiencing their grief.

With this method of avoidance, you have little control over what is happening and when. At any given time, you might feel overcome with emotions. You might even become fearful of when this is going to happen and how you will further postpone your grieving. This is an exhausting way to live and is not a sustainable lifestyle that anyone should have to endure. You already have a limited supply of energy as it is, so there is no need to further drain yourself by doing this.

Understandably, you might not feel like you have a choice in the matter. When grief tries to enter your life, it can become an automated response to procrastinate dealing with it. Always remember that you have a choice; you can make a small change in your life that will completely change the way you feel. It takes strength and bravery to move forward in this way, but you can do this. Give yourself the necessary motivation, and seek inspiration from others who have also been in your situation.

If you do not seek help or make a change, this type of avoidance pattern can evolve into serious depression or other mental health issues. Feeling the weight of long-term depression is going to make your grieving period even harder. Realize that you deserve better than this and that there are always resources for you to seek. If you do not know where to begin, you can always visit your local medical professional for guidance. They will be able to create an actionable plan full of steps that you can take.

The Displacer

This type of avoidance is complex because you go through the stages of grief as expected. You might experience strong emotions, such as anger or sadness, but you will direct them toward other people instead of addressing them on your own. When you do this, you are a displacer. The correct way to handle these emotions is to apply them to the person you are grieving, even the most difficult ones. This is how you are going to be able to sort through them properly.

A few things happen when you misdirect emotions toward other people. You might end up pushing people away who truly care about you. Even if you secretly do want their support, your emotions are going to tell you otherwise. They might make you act out of character in an attempt to self-isolate. You might also anger or upset the good people you have in your life. When you are feeling such intensity and directing it at other people, remarks often get taken to heart. Whether you mean to or not, you might end up hurting someone's feelings.

Keep in mind that this type of avoidance pattern can happen subconsciously or consciously; you might know exactly when you are doing this, or you might never realize it. Being mindful is going to help you in either case. When you are more aware of your actions, you can pick up on the cues that will tell you when you are doing it. If someone is upset or offended by your behavior, think about whether or not they have done anything to wrong you or hurt you. It is often the pain you feel from your grief that likes to lash out at people who love you unconditionally. Subconsciously, your brain is okay with this because they know that these people are supposed to care about you no matter what.

Even if you are not taking your anger out on other people, when you experience this kind of avoidance, you might feel constantly agitated about the smallest things. Every inconvenience is going to feel like a personal attack. If this happens, it will become difficult for you to enjoy your life. This can result in excessive complaining and can often end up pushing others away. You tend to become so self-focused that you forget to check in with those you care about. Any connection that you have in your life is a two-way street, and it takes mutual effort to maintain each one. This avoidance pattern almost makes you feel selfish, but you also feel like you cannot help it.

To reverse this feeling that you have inside, you should set a focus on self-care. When you begin caring about your well-being, the bad feelings you have inside should lessen. Bringing peace and clarity into your life can work wonders for your healing process. It might be uncomfortable to be kind to yourself, especially when you are feeling extremely agitated, but be patient with the process. Think about feeling better, not just right now but also in the long run.

The Substituter

This is a complex form of avoidance because it can happen in stages. You had a unique bond with the person you lost, whether they were your friend, family member, or romantic partner. When you experience the substitute avoidance pattern, you take all of the feelings and emotions you had for the person you lost and transfer them to someone else in your life. This is a hasty way to build any kind of relationship, and it can come off strong to the other person.

You might be so used to certain interactions and moments with the one you lost that they are programmed into your muscle memory. Since you have such a strong urge to continue the routine, you will try to find the next best person to try to have this bond with. By no means are you trying to replace your lost loved one; you are trying to find an outlet for the fondness you are left with. Instead of accepting that this person is gone and the routines you used to have are no more, you will do everything in your power to continue with them. Of course, you know that routines provide you with comfort and safety, which is why the decision is often hasty.

To prevent yourself from falling into this pattern, you can follow the three C's: companionship, commonality, and commitment. This is a good guideline to follow if you notice that you are growing closer to certain individuals in your life. You are probably leaning on them because they provide you with companionship, which can end up being a positive thing. Once you realize you have someone like this in your life, you need to determine if you have anything in common. Is the common link healthy?

Finally, your commitment to this person must be equally matched. This means that the feelings should be reciprocated. If you are invested in a relationship of any kind and the other person is not, you are bound to end up getting hurt. Not only will you feel betrayed when you realize you are putting more effort into the relationship, but you will also be hurtled through the process of grieving your lost loved one when you realize that you cannot simply substitute people to stand in for them.

Accepting that they are gone is hard. It makes sense that your brain would seek out substitution as a valid solution, but you need to consider the real reason behind why you are doing this—remind yourself of the three C's.

When you are substituting as a way of avoidance, you might end up convincing yourself that you are not being as strongly impacted by the loss of your loved one as you thought you would be. This can provide you with a sense of security and control. If there seems to be little risk of being overwhelmed, then you will often continue with the behavior that gives you this security.

The Decreaser

The main goal of this type of avoidance is to decrease the amount of grief that is felt. This can feel like a positive thing at first, but it becomes unhealthy when you end up never processing or addressing your true feelings. There are various techniques that you can rely on to use the act of decreasing your grief as a way of avoidance. People who fall into this pattern will normally become faith-based as they navigate through their grief. They will often find themselves praying, even bartering with the higher power that they believe in. What they seek is strength to overcome the grief and a way to decrease the level of intensity.

One of the main negative elements of this type of avoidance is that you might lead yourself to believe that you are okay, even without cycling through all of the stages of grief. Since you have faith in a higher power and feel that you are being heard, you might not want to seek out other help or treatment for your grief because you believe it is shortly coming to an end. Remember, grief ends with acceptance. This process can last for many years after you experience the loss, and it can continue for the rest of your life whenever you think about the person you lost.

Another worrisome outcome of this avoidance pattern is that people on the outside will think that you are doing fine. They might even be surprised that you are coping so well and believe that you do not need as much support as you do. Putting on a brave face like this is not always going to benefit you in the long run. This is just another way of putting off the inevitable. You need to address all of the moments you experience, even the weak ones.

Using rationalization is a big part of this avoidance pattern. Because you can see that your pain and sadness are decreasing, you might use this as an excuse to stop talking about your feelings or the loss. A little rationalization can be beneficial, but when you are insistent on it, it only fuels your avoidance even more. You can use your rational brain to understand that you aren't going to feel sad forever; there are ways you can find to pick yourself back up. It goes beyond rationalization when you believe that you are invincible or that you do not need any more help.

When it comes down to it, every step of the grieving process is important. You need to go through the hardship of grief to get the full picture of how to survive it. While you are healing, you aren't supposed to feel like you already know how to do everything. Even if you have experienced loss in the past, each one is unique. The whole process is personal, and it should be treated as such.

The Hypochondriac

This is a serious avoidance pattern that you might be unaware of because it tends to be rare. The definition of a hypochondriac is a person who has an intense fear surrounding their health and whether or not they are okay. A slight physical pain can appear as a glaring sign that something is wrong with them. How is this relevant to grief, though? Your feelings of grief can transform from emotional hardship into mock pain. You might be 100% convinced that you are injured, sick, or dying as well. It is a scary situation to find yourself in, especially because you will not be able to see past the anxiety when you are in the moment.

Naturally, becoming a hypochondriac is consuming. Feeling that you are constantly in pain becomes a huge distraction that you will not be able to ignore. Pretty soon, it will take over your entire life. Because other people might not understand what you are going through, they will trivialize your pain or brush it off. This results in you feeling even more hurt and angry because what you are experiencing is real to you. These symptoms feel just as real as any other you have felt in your life.

You might begin to isolate yourself from certain people because they do not take your symptoms as seriously as you'd like. While you do not want the attention for the sake of being seen, you do want people to care about you as you are experiencing these various ailments. The worst part is that you feel like nothing you can do will change the way you feel. No matter what, you still feel the pain and anxiety of what might happen to you. It is unsettling, and it can happen quickly.

Grief does have certain physical symptoms associated with it, and these will become your reasoning for believing that you have something seriously wrong with you. Each time you feel an inkling of physical discomfort, you will focus on it and run with it. As you can see, this becomes a way to distract yourself because you are so worried about your health. It completely bypasses any need to think about the loss you have just endured or how to process it.

These symptoms should never be dismissed. If you are truly worried about the state of your health, seek professional help immediately. In cases like this, it is much better to be safe than sorry. Getting a professional opinion may or may not help with your hypochondria, but it will be a step in the right direction. Sometimes, all it takes is validation to start feeling better. When a doctor acknowledges that you are experiencing the symptoms you say you are, it might be easier for you to begin processing them and figuring out what to do next.

As mentioned, these are only some of the most common avoidance patterns during grief. You might experience others that have not been mentioned. The most important part is to pay attention to any patterns that arise. With the knowledge that you now have on healthy versus unhealthy coping behaviors, you should be able to distinguish when you are doing something considered out of character as you attempt to seek comfort during this difficult time. The sooner you get help for these behaviors, the sooner you will begin to feel better.

6

DEALING WITH ANGER WHILE GRIEVING

F eeling anger after you experience a loss is incredibly common. You already know that it happens to be a stage of grief, and it can appear at any time during the process. The level and type of anger you feel is going to be personal depending on how you lost the person. If your loved one died in a car accident, you might resent the other driver who was responsible for the wreck. If your loved one died of an illness in the hospital, you might have a hatred for the doctors that were caring for them at the time. There are so many ways that your anger can take over because it is so powerful.

In this chapter, you will learn how to face your anger and deal with it.

UNDERSTANDING ANGER

Your anger manifests from a place that is much deeper than you think. Yes, you are angry that your loved one is gone, but there is often a lot more to it than this. You might begin to question yourself as you feel an increase in anger as you are grieving. Where is this coming from? How can it be stopped? The best way to figure out a solution to your anger is by locating the source of it. Think deeper than the loss of your loved one. Being as specific as you can, narrow in on why you are so angry. Maybe you feel anger because you wish you could have done more to help this person when they were alive. Perhaps you had plans with this person that will no longer be accomplished.

There is usually always a deeper meaning, but it can take some time to access it. To better understand the anger you are feeling, ask yourself what it is about the situation that is hurting you or making you afraid. The answer is usually going to revolve around one or more of your basic survival needs. These are love, shelter, hunger, identity, affiliation, and security. When this person died, how many of your basic needs were threatened? You might be able to pinpoint just one, or you might feel that all of them have been affected. No matter how you are feeling, it is valid. Take note of the ways that this loss has changed your life.

After a death, there is usually a follow-up that comes with a set of changes. You might have to change your living situation, or the way that your friends and family interact with you might differ. Each change that occurs will naturally make you feel off-balance. The feeling of security that you once had is in the process of evolving, but you might mistake it for being completely taken away from you. Hence, the anger will start to set in. Nobody wants to feel discomfort willingly. Most of us experience a great deal of security because we have familiarity with our lives. Losing someone can make it seem like nothing will ever feel familiar again.

After you lose someone, venting can come naturally. This can serve as both a healthy and unhealthy coping mechanism to guide you through the stages of grief. By getting these strong emotions off your chest, you are probably going to feel better. There can be a lot of unresolved anger resting until you finally vent to someone you trust. Be cautious of who you choose to vent to and how much you are venting, though. In any relationship, there must be a mutual give-and-take. This means that if you are only seeking out the company of others when you want to vent your anger and frustration, they are probably going to start feeling taken for granted.

Though you are going through a big loss in your life, time passes, and feelings can be hurt. When you only reach out to people to vent without asking them how they are doing too, you create an imbalance in the relationship. This can happen with your friends, family members, and a significant other. No matter who this person is, you are close to them for a reason. Remain mindful that they have events and situations going on in their lives too. In fact, it might be helpful to stop and listen to what they'd like to vent about at times. When you hear about other problems that others face, you might feel less alone while you move through the process of grieving.

If there is a lot of unresolved anger, your venting sessions might be misinterpreted. Your anger will rise to the surface, and the person you are venting to might mistakenly believe you are angry with them for some reason. This can cause tension and strain on the relationship, pushing this person out of your life. When this happens, it is upsetting because you likely do not know why it is happening or how it got to this point. Try to reel in your anger as you are venting, being mindful of the fact that this person did not take your loved one away from you. There are probably many people in your life who would love to listen to you talk about anything for any length of time, so make sure you are appreciating them.

If you do lash out at a person you care about, you might want to tuck yourself away or avoid them because you do not want to have to face them. An apology is never something you will regret, so make sure you apologize when you are in the wrong.

You might realize that venting to your friends isn't going to satisfy your need to talk about the loss and why you are feeling so much anger. In this case, you should look into grief counseling. Many people are resistant to the idea at first because they are convinced that they do not need help. There is nothing wrong with getting help, though. The resources are available to you for a reason. If you can find a grief counselor and group meetings in your area, consider trying them out. Because they are in a more professional setting, you will get the chance to express your deepest emotions while also hearing about what strangers are going through. This can become an eye-opening experience that might end up helping you heal.

By listening to the struggles of others, it is easier to pinpoint what you still have to be grateful for. There are so many ways that you are still lucky and still destined to live a happy and full life, even if it does not seem this way right now. Anger can cloud your judgment, but it will not be like this forever. The sooner you become aware of your actions and start taking responsibility for them, the better you will feel.

Bring Awareness Back Into Your Life

After experiencing anger because of your loss, you might end up with feelings of guilt or unresolved thoughts. Try not to punish yourself for feeling this way because you can make a change for the better. Becoming more self-aware will rebalance your thoughts. If you want to apologize to those around you for acting out due to your emotions, do so, and they will likely understand and accept your apology. Work on bringing awareness into your life so that you do not lose control of your emotions when interacting with others.

The following are some tips on how to bring more awareness back into your life when you are ready to resolve your anger:

- **Ask for Feedback**: If you don't know if you are being too harsh, ask someone you trust. The answer may not be easy for you to accept, but you will hear an honest outside perspective. Acknowledging and accepting constructive criticism can help you to be the best version of yourself. Even while you are mourning, it is encouraged to work on your characteristics and flaws. There is never going to be a shortage of coping skills to learn and traits to adopt that will make you feel better.
- **Learn Something New**: Anger tends to appear more frequently when you are micromanaging other people and what they are doing. This type of coping mechanism can appear based on your need to feel like you have control. Because you could not control the loss of your loved one, you will try anything to feel like you are regaining this control.

By teaching yourself something new, whether it be a new word each day or a new hobby, you can healthily feel like you are in control again.

- **Identify Inaccurate Thoughts**: When you are acting out of anger, you are likely to have irrational thoughts. These are identifiable based on their lack of supporting details. For example, if you feel that all of your friends dislike you now because you have been sad due to your loss, give yourself some reasons as to why this is not true. You might discover that your friends still check on you, want to spend time with you, and want to make sure that you heal from your loss. All of these signs point to a different conclusion, and it is important to be aware of this. Your mind can be your worst nightmare if you let these irrational thoughts take over. It can trigger anger inside of you that does not need to exist in the first place.

- **Clarify Your Values**: Your entire life has just changed because of this loss, and it is okay to admit that you feel this in a big way. When you no longer know what to focus on, it is common to experience anger and frustration. You can get back to your true self by reidentifying the things that matter most, like your current values. These values are personal, and you do not have to share them with anybody if you are uncomfortable. Simply restate your values to yourself to give you an idea of who you are as a person. Having this reassurance will make you feel confident and secure again.

- **Pay Attention to Triggers in Others**: You might feel like you are okay with who you are as a person, but it is other people that you find yourself frustrated with. This anger still stems from a trigger. Try to identify what triggers you in the behavior of other people. It is likely that their behavior either reminds you of yourself or your flaws; this is why it is bothering you so much. You might find that you are taking your anger out on others when, in reality, you are simply angry at yourself because you can identify with their weaknesses.

- **Meditate on Angry Thoughts**: When you feel like you can no longer cope with your anger or discuss it, meditate on it. Sit down in a quiet room with these thoughts, allowing them to manifest in the way that they need to. This will become an enlightening process for you, likely to highlight the true root of your problem. When you give yourself some solitary moments of thinking, you'll be surprised by what comes up.

ANGER CAN BE GOOD

Every negative emotion comes with a silver lining. There are some instances where your anger can be a positive thing. Some believe anger is an essential part of the grieving process. Without experiencing it, you might not fully heal.

There is not necessarily a "right" way to get angry, but there are ways to tell when the anger is healthy and improving your state of being. You can use your anger as a tool to help you get through your hardships. When you learn how to recognize and redirect it, you are reclaiming your power. To fully experience the best your anger has to offer, you need to be honest with yourself. When you are feeling angry, do not deny or stifle the feeling. Accept it because you must accept it before you can understand it.

Once you have learned how to recognize these moments, do not take immediate action. You need to see how the feeling is going to manifest. If you rush to stop it, you might be hindering yourself. Work with the feeling until it leads you to some point of action. The action is either going to be destructive, healthy, or neutral. If it is harmful to you or those around you, then you can intervene. When you feel it for a healthy or neutral reason, it is best to simply let the anger play out. Let all of the emotions go, willingly releasing them by using coping mechanisms you have learned.

The better you become at this self-identification process, the better you can communicate with others when you are feeling bad. If you know that you are angry and it is not the other person's fault, stating that you feel angry or upset can help to ease some of the tension that is building. You can tell them that it is not their fault but still warn them of the fact that you feel this way. This provides your loved ones with insight. They might not have known that you were feeling this way, but hearing it directly from you will offer them clarity.

You might not be willing to accept their kind words or gestures of help right now, and this is okay. If you feel that your loved ones are being too involved or overbearing when you are angry, communicate with them. Tell them that you would prefer to work through the issues alone but that you appreciate the support. This is a clear and concise way to express yourself without feeling like you are being backed into a corner. Having this newfound clarity should resolve a lot of the anger that might be unintentionally taken out on those who are trying to help you. Anyone who loves and respects you will be willing to back off as long as you are not in danger.

With your defensiveness at bay, your mind will feel clearer to seek solutions. This experience will show you that your anger can lead to a positive outcome. The more that you experience this, the less you will feel the need to suppress your anger. It can still be okay, even on the days when you feel the rage inside. You are going to have your ups and downs, but this is just a part of the entire grieving process, as you know. Work with these moments, being patient with yourself every step of the way. It may help to imagine that your best friend or most cherished loved one was going through the same thing. How would you treat them? When you can apply this same kindness to yourself, you will start to feel better.

What this experience all comes down to is, once again, realizing what you can and cannot control. If you are angry over something that cannot be changed, you need to realize that there is no traveling backward in time. You need to keep looking ahead, but that does not mean you cannot make changes right now that will improve the present. When you live in the moment, you will start to seek better solutions. You can use the anger that you feel like a passion to apply these changes in your life. Let it motivate you and guide you along the way. Working with your anger is just like working with any other emotion you feel. The more familiar you become with its patterns, the better you will become at comforting yourself.

Slow down when you begin to feel the anger rising in your chest. Acting on your anger can often result in an expedited feeling that will then lead to that out-of-control type of response. Take a few deep breaths when you start feeling overwhelmed; it helps more than you think. Realize that, more often than not, you are not being pressured or timed regarding your decision-making. You can take the time to work through your anger before you decide how you want to react. The rash decisions you make are the ones that you usually regret. We have all said things out of anger that we wish we hadn't, and these moments could have probably been avoided if we had just taken a moment to slow down.

Even when someone is standing in front of you and waiting for a response, you do not need to jump right in. Explain that you need a minute, and emotionally remove yourself from the situation. Even pausing for a short amount of time can help you to figure out what you need to say or do next. It is also okay if you do not know what must be done. Be honest with that person, and explain to them if you need more time to think or to be with your thoughts. Everyone heals at a different rate, and you do not need to feel guilty that you cannot instantly make decisions when you are angry. It takes a lot of patience and self-control to harness your emotions until you can think clearly. This skill will help you out in many ways throughout your life.

To better help yourself recognize when you need to stop, pause, or slow down, you can use this "speed limit" guide to help:

90 MPH	Explosive, violent
85 MPH	Fuming, outraged
80 MPH	Infuriated, enraged
75 MPH	Irate, exasperated
70 MPH	Bitter, indignant
65 MPH	Pissed off
60 MPH	Mad, angry
55 MPH	Agitated, perturbed
50 MPH	Annoyed, frustrated
45 MPH	Displeased, ruffled
40 MPH	Peaceful, tranquil

When using this guide, check in with yourself often. After you locate the emotions you are feeling, you can apply a "speed" to your level of anger. Next, you must decide what your speed limit is. What speed will you reach that requires some kind of intervention? Most people can handle minor annoyances and frustration, but there is no standard speed limit, especially when you are grieving. Keep in mind that your speed limit can also change as you heal. Once it is set, you can monitor your emotions, ensuring you are staying within this self-declared comfort zone.

Make a plan for what you will do if you start speeding. The most logical thing to do in any case is to slow down. By taking a moment to yourself to breathe or by engaging in a healthy coping behavior, you should be able to slow down your rate of anger. Using this chart can become a helpful way for you to manage your anger any time it surfaces.

You can also use visualization to help enforce your speed limit. Imagine that you are being pulled over when you notice that you are speeding. How fast were you going? Think about this as a warning that you are giving to yourself. Without punishing yourself for speeding, take this warning to heart, and consider what you can do to slow down and take better care of yourself. If you find yourself speeding again, think about getting pulled over one more time. In this case, you might need to make an active change to prevent yourself from going over the speed limit.

Removing yourself from your current environment can be a helpful way to manage your anger. If you are stewing in your negative feelings for a long time, these feelings are going to linger where you are. Going on a walk around the block can help tremendously, for example, because you are encouraging yourself to get out and experience a change in the atmosphere. You are going to be sensitive to other energy around you when you are dealing with anger. Pick up on the positive energy that you notice, using it as fuel to motivate you to head in a more positive direction. Spending time with people who are uplifting or spending time in nature are two ways that you can get the energetic recharge that you are craving.

Many people struggle with managing their anger, even before they lose a loved one. It is such a powerful emotion, and it might seem like you have no choice but to give in. Now, you are equipped with tools that you can use to fight back. Do not give in the instant that you feel your anger approaching. Understand it and realize that it is happening. Acknowledge it just as you would with your happiness and joy. This is how you are going to use it in a positive and healthy way.

The journey won't always be easy, but it will be worth it.

HOW TO COPE

You will learn which coping skills work best for your anger during this time. It is a good idea to start journaling so you can keep track of when you usually feel angry and why. Write down how you are feeling each day to spot any patterns in your behavior. This is going to help you cope well and adjust to this stage of grief that you must work through. Write down all of the coping mechanisms you try as well. Just because one does not seem to work on certain triggers does not mean it won't work on others. Anger can evolve, just like any other emotion. Being mindful of this, the following are some coping mechanisms to give you ideas of the kinds of behaviors you can try that might end up being successful for you.

Count Down

The next time you feel your anger rising, start counting. You can count down from 100 until you feel like your anger is subsiding. This seems like a simple coping mechanism because it is. It provides your brain with just enough of a distraction to redirect your thoughts. You might end up realizing that you aren't as angry about the situation as you thought you were. Once you feel like your anger is manageable, you can stop counting to regroup. Consider what can be done and what your end goal is. This will promote a focus on positive coping mechanisms.

Walk

Whether you go outdoors or into the next room, walking will provide you with a small dose of endorphins. These are the happy chemicals that result from participating in physical activity. Walk around until you can feel your anger subsiding. While this is not going to cure the anger that you feel or the situation you are experiencing, it will lessen the severity of it. This will result in a more manageable feeling that will allow you to regain control of your behaviors.

Relax Your Muscles

Because anger is an emotion, you might not even think that it can create physical ailments. But holding a lot of tension inside brings you symptoms such as muscle soreness, stomach pain, and headaches. Taking a long, hot bath can help to relax your muscles when you are angry. Even simply lying down for a few moments and working on muscle isolations can improve your state of mind. To do this, close your eyes and imagine that you are relaxing your body from the tips of your toes to the top of your head. Work your way up until you have fully relaxed all of your muscles.

Recite a Mantra

Using a mantra is like relying on a certain word or phrase to inspire you throughout the day. Your mantra can be anything that uplifts you. "I will get through this" is an example of something general and applicable to almost every situation. When you are feeling angry and like you are about to reach your breaking point, breathe and recite your mantra in your head. If possible, recite it out loud to yourself in the mirror. The goal is to say it enough that you convince yourself of the positive affirmation you are repeating.

Mentally Escape

Using visualization to leave your situation for a moment can help the anger subside. Close your eyes and imagine the most relaxing place you can think of. This place might be somewhere you've been before or it might only exist in your mind. No matter where you go, tell yourself that your anger cannot follow you here; this is a safe space. Think about what the area looks and sounds like. Are there other people with you or are you there by yourself? Try to think about all of the smallest details as they will start to add up and bring positivity into your life.

Play Some Music

The power of music can be healing. When you notice that your mood is declining, play your favorite songs. It helps to have a playlist handy for when these moments occur. By hearing the familiar and welcoming tunes, you are naturally going to lighten up. The power of music can be transformative, often taking you to different places mentally. Allow yourself to get lost in each song, listening to the beat, the instruments, and the lyrics. If you feel compelled, you can even dance as you feel each tune.

Stop Talking

Hearing your own words being projected can often trigger your anger. You are already feeling frustrated, so stop trying to over-explain yourself or defend your feelings. Instead, take the time to do the opposite.

Oftentimes, the source of your anger will make its appearance during this silence. Welcome it if this happens. The silence can be scary sometimes, but you can learn to use it as a tool to get to the bottom of your negativity.

Take Action

Even if you are not working directly on solving the problem, you can harness your anger in other ways. Use it to stir up the passionate side of you. If there is a cause that you can contribute to, do so. This can make you feel productive and will be a useful way to unleash this energy. When you feel that your contributions matter, you are going to be momentarily satisfied. This temporary relief from your anger can help you to calm down and move forward.

Select an Immediate Solution

You already know that there are many things you can do to take action when you are experiencing anger. Out of all of the solutions you come up with, rank them from the most immediate to the most time-consuming. When you can pick a solution that provides you with immediate relief, you are going to feel a lot better. Not to be confused with instant gratification, this solution for your anger should still revolve around healthy coping mechanisms and lasting positive effects.

Picture a Stop Sign

This is another coping skill that seems trivial, but it can help you by being a direct reminder. As you feel yourself approaching the edge of your anger, imagine a big stop sign in front of you. Picture it clearly, red with bold font. Use this as a chance to take caution before you reach an explosive level of anger. Sometimes, you need to provide yourself with the warning signs before your mind is trained to do so on its own. You need to condition yourself to learn that there are consequences for making rash decisions.

Change Your Routine

Aspects of your routine can lead to annoyance and frustration. From the traffic that you encounter on your drive to work to the other inconveniences you face, your anger can reach its tipping point when you never make any changes to your routine. After a loss, changing your routine can feel refreshing. Drive a different route, and make your life easier during this time. This will help with your anger, and it can also help to make life feel less stressful.

Laugh

You might feel like you don't have many reasons to laugh nowadays, but the cliché is true; laughter can feel like the best medicine when you are down. If nothing comical is making you laugh, try laughing at nothing. This might feel odd, but it is going to release happy chemicals in your brain that will promote the state of your well-being. You might end up really laughing because you feel funny for making yourself laugh. Try to watch funny movies or listen to amusing stories.

During this time, you want to promote as much uplifting energy in your life as you can.

Practice Gratitude

The next time you feel like you are about to lash out in anger, try stopping and writing down three things that you are grateful for. They can be people, traits, objects, or anything that reminds you that you are still lucky. Putting things into perspective like this will teach you that there is still so much in your life to appreciate. When you lose someone you love, it can feel like life isn't worth living anymore. You need to give yourself consistent reminders that there are always going to be silver linings, as long as you seek them.

Set a Timer

Whenever you are feeling an urge to act on your anger, set a timer for five minutes. Before you respond based on how you are feeling, allow this time to pass without taking any action. You don't have to think about anything in particular, but pay attention to the way you are feeling. You'd be surprised how much these feelings can change if you simply allow some time and space between your thoughts and actions. Evaluate if you still want to act out in the way that you originally did once the timer goes off. This exercise will serve as a reminder that you need to be more patient with yourself to healthily process what you are feeling.

Write a Letter

When somebody triggers your anger, you cannot always speak your mind at the moment. Instead, write everything down in a letter to said person. Without censoring yourself, write down all of the things that are bothering you and why. Pretend that you are saying them directly to the person you feel angry with. After you are finished, read the letter. Feel the anger leaving your mind and body as it transfers onto the page. Make a point to keep reading what you have written until you feel like the anger has left you. Then, get rid of the letter. You can throw it away, rip it up, burn it, or do anything that feels good to you. This is a symbolic way to get your negativity out, and it allows you to vent about what you are going through without causing any conflict or tension.

Find Freedom

Sometimes, you are going to feel angry, yet you are going to be the one who is in the wrong. Understand that it is never beneath you to apologize when you make a mistake. Find freedom in the process of taking accountability for your actions. Nobody is perfect, yourself included. Having the power to recognize that you have made a mistake and that you care about another person's feelings enough to apologize is a great trait to maintain. Feel proud of yourself for doing the right thing and allowing the anger to be set free through your apology.

These are only some of the ways that you can practice to cope with your anger. As you explore them, you will find other ways that might end up working better for you. Anger is a personal emotion as not everyone is triggered by the same events and situations. Also, not everyone is experiencing a loss like you are. Be mindful of the entire process, even the parts that are difficult to manage. Through these healthy expressions of anger, you will slowly release it from your mind and body. Remind yourself that this is only one of the stages of grief that you must get through. Eventually, the way you feel is going to evolve.

It might shock you how much your temper flares up during this time, but try not to be so hard on yourself; you are not the same version of yourself you once were. Loss is traumatic, and trauma can change people. While you might never be the same version of yourself as you once were, you can certainly find your way back to your core values.

Imagine what the most important things in your life are right now. Even if you can only think of one or two of them, this gives you an excellent foundation to live your life. Make what is important to you a priority. This means setting new goals and striving to be better for whatever it is that you value. You might feel lost and confused right now, but that moment of clarity will come for you.

7

HOW TO USE THE WIM HOF METHOD TO DEAL WITH GRIEF

W im Hof has completed some impressive accomplishments in his lifetime. He is a Dutch athlete and a 26-time world record holder at 61 years old. Hof claims that he can control his nervous system with his own will thanks to his special training model. The model allows him to withstand both physical and mental extremes, and others who follow it can control their nervous systems as well. The Wim Hof Method mainly consists of breathing exercises and exposure to the elements that are thought to help you reclaim more conscious control than you have ever had before.

But how does this relate to dealing with grief? Well, grief tends to do the opposite; it makes you lose consciousness and touch with reality as you are sucked into your emotions. As we discussed before, being aware of how you feel can help you when you are stuck in your grief.

Unfortunately, Hof himself is familiar with grief. In 1995, he lost his wife to suicide, leaving him to raise their four children on his own. An unimaginable hardship, he struggled to work through the stages of grief and balance the many responsibilities placed on his shoulders. He knew that he had to become mentally stronger if he was going to survive, not only for his sake but to honor his wife and to raise their children.

This need to be strong led Hof to create his Wim Hof Method. While it is something unconventional that you probably never imagined trying before, it has been beneficial in his own life and with the ailments that he has faced while grieving.

While reading about this method, remain mindful of the fact that this all stemmed from the hardship of loss. Just as you are struggling right now, Hof also experienced his own struggle. You are not alone when you are feeling at your absolute lowest point. Hof reached this point during his period of grief, but he was able to overcome it through a lot of self-discipline. This is the only way that you are going to be able to rewire your brain and heal yourself, or so Hof believes.

In this chapter, the method will be expanded to give you a clear understanding of what it takes to gain complete control of your nervous system. In turn, this will help you cope with your grief in a proactive way. While the method might feel intense to you, there are ways to safely transition into it to get your mind and body used to these changes.

Although the Wim Hof Method is not a guaranteed way to free you from the constructs of your grief, it will allow you to make a solid attempt. As you are searching for answers and feeling confused during your grief, committing yourself to something immersive might be exactly what it takes to give yourself an extra boost of strength.

THREE BASIC PRINCIPLES

The Wim Hof Method consists of three different parts: controlled hyperventilation, exhalation, and retention. This can sound overwhelming at first, but these principles are broken down into steps to allow you to achieve them without much difficulty. You will also become better at them as you train, much like an athlete improves their performance.

As an athlete, Wim Hof was used to rigorous training and goal-setting, so he incorporated these values into his method. He understands that you are not going to simply feel better overnight after you use this method one time. You need to be consistent with it, and you need to practice if you want to see an improvement.

Let's start with hyperventilation, which is when you breathe more rapidly than normal.

At first, the idea of hyperventilation sounds negative. You likely associate it with panic and feeling uneasy. Going through grief, there are likely moments when you experience it in a negative way. A lot of people hyperventilate when they first find out the terrible news that they have lost a loved one because it is a programmed response that happens when your brain does not know how to process the information it has received. Part of the Wim Hof Method is taking back the power from the things that make you powerless, and your breathing is one of them. It is no secret that your breath can be controlled. This has been practiced since ancient times in yoga. By controlling your breathing, you are regulating your mind and body.

To begin the Wim Hof Method, use the following steps:

1. Take 30 powerful breaths in a row, inhaling deeply to fill the lungs.
2. Passively release the air from your lungs, allowing it to escape naturally. After you have released it, hold your breath for 1 to 3 minutes or as long as you can.
3. Take another deep inhale and hold for 15 to 20 seconds before releasing the breath.

As you repeat this exhalation process, you should begin to feel a slight tingling in your arms and legs. This is a sign that you are doing it correctly. Feeling slightly lightheaded is also normal. You must be careful as you begin to practice controlled hyperventilation because it can be dangerous to disrupt your breathing too consistently. You must always practice this in a seated, controlled position. Never hyperventilate while you are in the bathtub or anywhere where you might fall and get injured.

When you first start the Wim Hof Method, you should not exceed 30 inhalations during a single session. This is going to be a lot on the average person's lungs. The idea is to give yourself a challenge but to avoid being detrimental to your mind and body. Once you have more experience, you might be able to withstand 60 inhalations, but your goal should not be to increase this number. Instead, focus on getting yourself to the point of a steady rhythm. After this, you can move on to the next step, which is exhalation. You will take a final inhalation as you are hyperventilating, and then you will focus on regulating your breath once more.

Your cycles are now complete, and it is time to fully exhale. As you do, let the air escape slowly and in a controlled fashion. This time, you are going to empty your lungs to breathe normally again. Imagine your entire body being revitalized now.

By completing these first two steps, you have changed the way that you are breathing in its entirety. The final step is retention. You are going to feel a strong urge to inhale once you complete your long exhalation. As soon as this happens and your lungs are empty, allow yourself to inhale deeply and hold this breath for 15 to 20 seconds. The goal here is not to make your breathing jagged again but instead to regulate it.

At this point, you might experience a head rush. Continue to remain seated for a few minutes after you complete this breathing exercise. If you feel the need, you can repeat the retention step up to three times. Be cautious of your lightheadedness.

Immediately after you finish the three basic steps, try getting into a cold shower. It should not feel as cold or jarring to you as it normally does, and this is because you have reset your nervous system. You might even feel like the water is warm and comfortable! It is incredible what you can do if you simply put your mind to it.

Wim Hof also encourages you to try to work out after you feel that you have regained your breath. The physical activity should not feel as strenuous as it normally does.

I do my breathe work in the shower and as soon as I'm finished, I crank the shower to cold and focus on my breathing. Be mindful that I have been doing this for a while and I'm able to stand while I do it. If you're new you may want to slowly expose yourself to cold water therapy by finishing your shower with a 15-30 second cold portion.

BENEFITS

The breathing exercise from the Wim Hof Method comes with several advantages. Because you are revitalizing the way you breathe, you are almost going to feel a surge in power. This type of breathing releases a big amount of energy, which is why you feel so recharged after completing it. It influences your nervous system and changes various physiological responses.

One of the biggest benefits is what the Wim Hof Method will do for your stress levels. When you practice the breathing exercise, you trigger what is known as the short stress response. This means that you will feel more resilient to the stressors that appear in your daily life.

You are probably familiar with the days where every stressor feels like it can break you down. This becomes especially true as you experience stress while grieving. Even the smallest inconvenience can feel like the end of the world. By practicing the Wim Hof Method, you are giving yourself more strength and protection against these stressors. The calmness and resilience that you feel will encourage you to believe that things will be okay again. This is important because the loss you are going through tends to make it seem like your sense of what is normal has been shattered.

Stress is not only detrimental to your mental health; it can also destroy your physical well-being. When you constantly live under the weight of your stressors, your body feels tired and worn down. You might not feel like you have enough energy to complete your normal tasks, which can lead to feelings of helplessness. As you know, this can often become a precursor to serious mental illnesses such as depression. Stress is not something that you should force yourself to live with. It is an ailment that can make any loss seem more painful and exaggerated, but you can lessen its effects when you control your breathing.

Having more control is a feeling that nearly every human craves. The things that happen to us in life are often going to be outside of our control, especially negative things. This is why our programmed responses are so important. As you practice the breathing exercise that Wim Hof provides, you are restoring your faith in your ability to control your responses. This is going to build you up and get you through even your hardest moments. Imagine what Wim Hof went through as he simultaneously grieved his lost wife and had to continue to raise their children. This unimaginable pain is something that you can probably relate to the loss of your loved one.

Another benefit of the Wim Hof Method is the ability to quickly recover from physical activity. Even if you are not running marathons and working out daily, your body is naturally going to feel more tired when you are grieving. Simple tasks will wear you out, but regulating your nervous system can help to rebalance the way you feel. In turn, this also impacts your ability to sleep; you will find it easier to fall asleep and will be able to get restful sleep. If you have been struggling with this since the loss, you will find a lot of relief. Getting a good night's sleep can change your entire outlook on your day ahead.

You might also discover that your creative brain has experienced a surge in activity. While creativity is not necessary during mourning, it can help you as a healthy coping mechanism. Being able to think outside of the box and to express yourself with creativity gives you something else to focus on other than the loss you have experienced. Take advantage of this benefit by attempting to do something creative on a regular basis. You can paint, draw, write, dance, sing, or do anything that feels good to you. This will become an uplifting part of your routine, and you will find it helpful in regulating your mood and emotions.

One of the best benefits of the Wim Hof Method is enhanced mental clarity. Grief puts you through a lot of uncertainty and doubt. You might be stuck on the idea that you don't know how to go on in life without your loved one or that you do not want to, but with a restored sense of clarity, you will find your way back to your core values. Your life will have meaning once again, and you might even feel motivated to create new goals for yourself. Starting small is not a bad thing. Even if you can only manage to work on one goal at a time, this is a step in the right direction. It will give you a sense of purpose and guidance that you need during this time.

Lastly, an interesting benefit of the Wim Hof Method is its ability to lower your symptoms and risk factors for certain diseases, such as arthritis, Parkinson's, asthma, and several autoimmune disorders. As we age and experience stress, the risk factors for many of these diseases increase. You can use the Wim Hof Method as a preventative measure against them. The last thing that you need is to fall ill or to struggle even more during this time. After all, part of the grieving process includes taking care of yourself as you simultaneously go through each stage.

SCIENCE

To better understand the Wim Hof Method and why it can provide you with all of the above benefits, it is essential to understand the science behind it. By breaking this down, you will have a clear idea of what is going on inside of your mind and body as you complete the breathing exercise.

Most people are familiar with the basic concept of why breathing deeply is so great for you. When we breathe, oxygen is inhaled, and carbon dioxide is exhaled. When carbon dioxide is in your system, it reacts with water to create carbonic acid. When your blood is more acidic, your ability to breathe slowly and regularly is impacted. You will find the need to take sharper, jagged breaths. Panic is more likely to happen as well. Overall, acidic blood means less stability as you cycle through your negative emotions.

The Wim Hof Method lowers your carbon dioxide levels since you are exhaling more deeply. This creates a more blanched pH level in your blood, which means that it is alkaline. According to researchers at Radboud University Medical Center, this is why you tend to experience the tingling in your limbs as you perform the Wim Hof Method

(Sinicki 2018). Your body goes into a state of "intermittent respiratory alkalosis," meaning your blood is alkaline as you control your hyperventilation. Making your blood more alkaline also means that you are preventing your body from properly using its oxygen stores. This can sound dangerous, but it prompts your body to "recycle" the oxygen instead of becoming dependent on new oxygen to breathe properly.

When you are holding your inhalation in the second step of the Wim Hof Method, the recycling process takes place. Without it, you would likely become too lightheaded and end up passing out. The carbon dioxide is recycled just enough when you hold your breath for the short period that you can take it in. This is why practicing more inhalations of controlled hyperventilation is never the goal. It becomes dangerous easily, and you do not want to overdo it.

Adrenaline

During the process of completing the Wim Hof Method, your body starts to create adrenaline. This is what is responsible for your fight-or-flight response and the feeling of wanting to take a deep breath. Part of this feeling is triggered by panic and your body's desire to breathe normally, but there is another part that is thought to be triggered by the vagus nerve. This is the longest of your cranial nerves, and its purpose is to monitor your bodily functions and processes. So, while your body might be entering its fight-or-flight response because the adrenaline has kicked in, it will also begin to be regulated by the vagus nerve. This nerve responds to many triggers, such as temperature, oxygen levels, the inner workings of your gut, and more.

Calm vs. Panicked

You might be wondering why it isn't more beneficial to just breathe deeply and calmly like in yoga and martial arts. When you breathe this way, your body is telling the parasympathetic nervous system that all is well. This lowers your heart rate and tells your body that it is okay to slow down and pay less attention to what is going on. With faster, panicked breathing, you experience hyper-focus and concentration. Since the parasympathetic nervous system is on alert that something might not be okay, it gives you a boost of energy to get through whatever it is that you are trying to overcome.

Some studies show it is healthy to stimulate the vagus nerve in this way when dealing with certain mental illnesses. Because grief can put you in such a downward spiral pattern, it is thought that you do not need to calm down to feel better. You need to completely change the way your body is operating, and giving yourself this sudden boost of energy can do just that.

Long-Term Effects

In simple terms, it has already been stated that you are temporarily making your blood more alkaline as you complete the Wim Hof Method, but what does this mean for the long-term? If you decide you'd like to regularly use this method to trigger responses in your body and receive benefits, you are also going to benefit from the production of more red blood cells. When your oxygen levels are reduced, EPO is secreted. EPO, or erythropoietin, is a hormone that is essential to the production of your red blood cells. If you are regularly reducing your oxygen levels, the EPO is going to spread throughout your body more frequently.

This means that you are also going to experience the ability to perform tasks that require more endurance. While you might not have any desire to become a professional athlete like Wim Hof, you already know how difficult average tasks feel as you are going through the hardship of your loss. Any boost in endurance is going to feel like some much-needed assistance, no matter what stage of grief you are in. This is thought to have a similar effect to high-altitude training. When athletes need to build their endurance, they train in places that have a higher altitude because it takes more energy to complete the same tasks. At a higher altitude, it becomes harder to breathe because the oxygen levels change.

Next, you must take into account the other part of the method—cold exposure. Your body is exposed to something normally shocking, but it can withstand the effects. In the long-term, this type of exposure is thought to train your immune system to become stronger. According to a study by the *European Journal of Applied Physiology and Occupational Physiology*, because of this exposure, the body learned how to raise lymphocytes, which are white blood cells that are found in the vertebrate immune system (Sinicki 2018). These cells are essential to your immune system.

Most people are under the misconception that exposure to the cold will make them sick. You probably grew up hearing from your parents to wear a jacket to avoid catching a cold. The reason why you end up getting sick after exposure to the cold is that you were already at risk. Since the cold suppresses your immune system, you become more vulnerable. With the ability to control your immune system and to make it stronger, you can experience colder elements without falling ill. When you repeatedly challenge your immune system by practicing the Wim Hof Method, it will continue to become stronger.

Key Scientific Studies

Below is a collection of additional studies done on the Wim Hof Method that back its benefits. Through this research, you will be able to better understand exactly what your body is going through and why it is seen as a positive change.

Radboud University, The Netherlands (2014)

- Focused on testing a larger group in the same way that they first tested Wim Hof back in 2011
- 12 practitioners of the Wim Hof Method were injected with endotoxin
- Results were similar to Wim Hof's—they were able to control their parasympathetic nervous system and boost their immune response
- Anti-inflammatory protection was 200%+ higher
- Conditions associated with inflammation, such as autoimmune disorders, were thought to see benefits if the upkeep of the method were to take place

Wayne State University, Michigan, United States (2018)

- The "Brain Over Body" study

- Focused on understanding brain function that allows Wim Hof to withstand extremely cold temperatures
- Wim Hof wore a temperature control suit and was placed in an MRI machine and a PET scan machine
- Results revealed his brain activated pain suppression

CONNECTION TO GRIEF

You have experienced sadness many times before, but the intensity of the sadness that your grief brings can feel different. In most cases of sadness, you can navigate your way through without much disruption to your routines and schedule.

However, because loss is so powerful, personal, and outside of your control, the sadness is going to feel a lot worse. You already know that this sadness can develop into clinical depression if left untreated. The longer that you feel sad, the more you are at risk of becoming clinically depressed. This is why some type of intervention becomes necessary. Without any treatment, you are left to struggle with your feelings of sadness on your own.

There are ways that the scientific benefits of the Wim Hof Method can help your sadness and depression. When you become clinically depressed, your blood becomes more inflamed. These higher amounts of inflammation are typically found in those who are struggling with chronic depression. Since the Wim Hof Method has been proven to lower these rates of inflammation in your body, it is going to help you overcome your sadness and depression from the inside out. On a physical level, there isn't much else that you can do to change your inflammation levels. This is what makes the method so powerful.

Wim Hof is a believer in holistic ways of healing, and the more natural the better. Besides going to therapy and seeking help this way, you can also work on taking certain actions at home that will allow your life to feel more carefree. These activities help you to fight the negative thoughts from the source as they are mind-focused. You will ultimately be able to overcome your sadness once you get to the root cause of your negativity.

While there are several natural healing options out there, below are some of the ones I recommend.

Meditation

There are tens of thousands of studies on meditation and how it is impactful when it comes to treating sadness and depression. The art of meditation has been practiced since ancient times, and it continues to be a favorite activity that is sought out by those who wish to take a holistic approach to healing.

There is no right or wrong way to meditate. The idea is that you must focus your mind on something positive and peaceful to prevent negative or sad thoughts from taking over. In some ways, the Wim Hof Method is like meditation because you are putting intense focus on your breathing.

To practice meditation in a more traditional sense, you have a few options. You can go to a meditation class that is led by a teacher, you can find a guided meditation online, or you can lead yourself through a self-guided session. Depending on your level of experience with meditation and your overall comfort, your choice will vary. Remember, any of these forms of meditation are going to be beneficial to you. As long as you have a private area to meditate that is quiet and peaceful, you will be able to make the most of your session.

When you are left alone with only your thoughts, which happens during meditation, it is unsurprising that the negative ones try to surface the fastest. Instead of suppressing these thoughts, give them the chance to form and acknowledge them. Do not hold on to them or try to fix them at the moment; instead, imagine that they are floating away on a running current of a river. As you envision each negative or sad thought being washed along the river, think about how this is making room for new thoughts. With time, the negative ones will eventually subside.

When you meditate, you can keep a mantra or a positive affirmation in mind. This is your intention that you are putting into your meditation session. Think of it as what you hope to achieve. A good starting point is peace or clarity. Grief can make you feel like you have lost both, so seeking more is going to benefit you at this point in your life. Much like any form of healing, you cannot expect to feel 100% better after you meditate once, but practice will make a difference. The idea is that you can make meditation a bigger part of your life, practicing it often. Just as there is no correct way to meditate, there is also no limit on how much you can meditate.

Most people choose to meditate either first thing in the morning or before bed. Usually, your mind is going to be clearest when you first wake up, so making time for meditation will get your day started on a positive note. Alternatively, meditating before bed becomes a great way to clear your mind, which will allow you to sleep better. You can even do both if you have the time and energy for it.

Physical Activity

Engaging in any type of physical activity while you are grieving is highly encouraged. Creating more endorphins in your brain allows you to feel happier. Working out or moving is probably one of the last things that you feel like doing as you are going through your grief, but getting past the initial resistance to it can help you. Commit to doing at least two to three different types of physical activity each week. These activities do not have to be complex or strenuous. Even just taking a walk around your neighborhood can be enough to release these endorphins and make you feel a lot better.

As an athlete, Wim Hof relied on endorphins to get him through his grief. While you don't need to be a super athlete like Wim Hof, being able to focus on something productive is going to benefit you. Knowing that doing something physical is not only healthy for you but can also present you with a set of goals can prove a much-needed sense of relief.

The following are some forms of physical activity that you can partake in when you feel like you need to get up and moving:

- Dancing
- Stretching
- Jogging
- Weight-lifting

- Doing chores
- Preparing meals
- Walking around your house

Do whatever you feel comfortable with, and remember that you might have to build up your will to complete these tasks in the beginning. Even if you can only manage to get up and walk around your room one time, this is still an improvement. You will get your legs moving and begin to feel a slight rush of endorphins in your brain.

Partaking in physical activities also promotes the growth of new brain cells. As they form, you will find that you can get a better night's sleep. This is essential for someone who is going through the grieving process. You will also feel an increase in your self-esteem, which has naturally suffered a blow since you have been dealing with so much uncertainty in your life during this time.

A great way to enhance this process is to perform your physical activity outside in the sunshine if possible. The added benefits that you get from receiving natural vitamin D will make you feel even happier. We all need vitamin D to live healthy lives, so making sure that you are getting enough of it during this time is more important than ever. Monitor the way you feel when you perform your physical activity indoors versus outdoors in the sunlight. You are guaranteed to feel a difference when you are done.

Support

It becomes so easy to withdraw from everyone in your life when you are experiencing the hardship of grief. Maybe you do not want to explain to other people how you are feeling, or maybe you do not want to talk about your loss any longer. No matter the cause, it becomes hard to think about spending time around other people, even if they have your best intentions in mind.

To make the idea of socializing less overwhelming, remind yourself that you do not have to socialize with everyone who wants to see you. As you are working through your feelings, realize that you can decide who you'd like to spend your time around. It is always a good idea to be around someone you already felt comfortable with before because this takes away a lot of the pressure of socialization. Since this person already knows you well, there will be less of a need to explain yourself or the way you are feeling. You will be able to simply spend time with them and feed off of their energy.

The people you choose to be close to during this time must be providing you with nothing but uplifting energy. You do not need any more bad energy right now, and if someone makes you feel this way, it is not selfish to temporarily distance yourself from them until you are feeling better. This is a process, and it will have many ups and downs. The people in your life, no matter how close you are, might not always know what you want or need during this period of healing. This is why it helps you express yourself as best as you can. Tell others what they can do for you as they are probably already there and willing to help you get through this.

Most people tend to feel selfish when they must ask for what they need, but this is not the case; knowing what you need to feel better only showcases your strength. It is not wrong for you to ask for love and support right now because you need it more than ever. Be kind to yourself, just as the people in your life are being kind to you. Listen to them talk about their lives and struggles. This change in conversation might help you by showing you different perspectives and other ways of life. It is a reminder that you are not alone in the fact that you are having a hard time, and other people are going through their version of the human experience.

Diet

What you eat matters because it becomes the fuel that keeps you going. When you are feeling sad and stressed, you might want to reach for your comfort foods. For most people, this means a lot of processed foods and sugars. Most of the time, junk food is considered a comfort food because it is convenient and artificially processed to taste good. Treating yourself to these things every once in a while is okay, but you need to make sure that you are maintaining a balanced diet overall. Seek out foods that are high in vitamins and nutrients to protect your mind and body. These are some essentials that you should be including in your diet during this time:

- Nuts
- Legumes
- Whole grains
- Dark leafy greens
- Eggs
- Salmon
- Dark chocolate
- Asparagus
- Broccoli

- Blueberries
- Strawberries
- Apples
- Plums
- Beans

By including more of these ingredients in your diet, you are providing yourself with more antioxidants, vitamins, and minerals that will keep your body going strong. They are also beneficial to your mind because they help you focus and think clearly.

When you eat junk food, you feel instant gratification because it tastes good. But because this type of food is not nutritious, you almost always experience some sort of crash after you eat it. This can be subtle, but it often tanks your energy levels, which can put you in an even worse mood.

You can treat yourself to your comfort foods sometimes, but make sure that a majority of your diet consists of whole foods and natural ingredients. These are going to feel especially rejuvenating to you right now. Over time, your body will begin to crave these foods instead of junk food. The more that you stop giving in to your cravings, the more you are promoting change. This does take self-disciple, but you have what it takes to ensure that you are taking better care of yourself during this time. Without a healthy mind and body, your inner systems will begin to deteriorate. Everything is going to start feeling harder and worse.

Grief can often take your hunger away entirely, but you must also use your self-discipline in this case. Even when you do not feel hungry, you need to make sure that you are keeping up with your basic levels of nourishment. The sadness can often mask the feeling of hunger, but your body is still going to feel it intensely. Over time, you are going to become weaker. Before this starts to happen to you, plan out a couple of your meals, and give yourself regular reminders to eat them. While you might not feel like eating a whole portion, getting something nutritious into your stomach is only going to help you during this time.

Part of grief is exploring your options, and this is exactly what the Wim Hof Method provides you—an option to take. It is something unconventional, but it can end up helping you if you are willing to give it a try.

Most people feel discouraged during grief because it feels like happiness is unattainable. This is what happens when you become stuck in your routines. Even when it is hard, try to become brave enough to branch out.

CONCLUSION

You have made it through this book, which means you have made it one step closer to feeling better. Now, use the techniques you have learned to support yourself daily. Re-read them as needed and think about how to incorporate each one into your life. Some moments are going to feel hard, and you are going to need to rely on the skills you gained from this book and the support from the people who you have around you.

Grief makes everything feel like a never-ending cycle, but you know now that this is far from true. Instead, grief comes in stages that you must learn how to navigate. Some days will feel profoundly difficult, but you can rely on your strength and new skills to get you through them. Knowing that you are not alone in these feelings and this experience helps to remind you that it is all going to be okay even if it doesn't feel that way. While nothing will ever replace the presence of the person you lost, there are ways to make sure that you are honoring their memory to the best of your ability.

The process of grief changes your life, often when you are least expecting a change. But you are not helpless, and you are not alone. After reading through the topics covered in this book, you will have the necessary strength and skills to reach your next stage of grief. But you need to remain open to the natural flow of the process and remember that you can be at any stage for any amount of time. Understand that this is a normal response to the stress that you are going through, and it will get better given time even if it feels unbearable now. You will be tested both physically and mentally, but in the end, you will be able to overcome all of your symptoms.

To overcome the grief, it will be necessary to respond with a balanced approach. You cannot entirely block out the loss or the pain because this will only suppress the negativity temporarily. Eventually, you will have to face it and work through it. With grief, it is always better to experience your feelings at the beginning of the process. Explore them, even if they make you uncomfortable. This is how you are going to learn what you need to work through them. There will be moments that test you and make you feel that you cannot go on, but you will find ways to overcome them. Grief puts you in a position where you must learn how to experience discomfort before you can feel normal again.

You will learn a lot about yourself during this process, and you will find ways to make yourself feel okay again. Remember that loss is a natural part of life, and grief is a healthy response to it. By recognizing the common patterns of grief, including all of the intense sadness and anger, you will be able to assure yourself that you are on the right path toward healing.

There are many things that you can do for yourself during this time to make the grief feel easier. Whether you want to explore Stoicism, the Wim Hof method, professional help, or other holistic activities, never stop believing in the fact that you will be able to feel okay again. You must be willing to give these a try, though. Even if it is something you have never done before, give it a go to see if it can help you.

With all of your tools in mind, the time to heal is now. Do not spend another moment suffering because of your loss. You can turn this time into one of transformation and growth. Use all of the resources you can, and follow your instincts. They will guide you through a lot of the pain and discomfort that arises.

If you enjoy what you have learned from this book, do not forget to leave a review. Tell others about your story and how much you have overcome so far. You can also read about other experiences that people have been through with their grief and trauma. Through inspiration from others, you will be able to gather even more strength to get you through this difficult time.

Feel free to add me on Instagram (@cortezranieri) and send me a DM with your story and how this book may have helped. If you haven't already, check out my first book, *10 Habits For Grief and Loss*. Thank you so much for taking the time to read this book, it means the world to me!

REFERENCES

10 Simple Ways to Improve Your Self-Awareness [With Examples]. *Nick Wignall*. (2020, October 29). https://nickwignall.com/self-awareness/.

The Benefits of Breathing Exercises: Wim Hof Method. The Benefits of Breathing Exercises | *Wim Hof Method*. https://www.wimhofmethod.com/breathing-exercises.

Cherry, K. (2019, July 17). How Attachment Theory Works. *Verywell Mind*. https://www.verywellmind.com/what-is-attachment-theory-2795337.

Cherry, K. (2020, March 29). How John Bowlby Influenced Child Psychology. *Verywell Mind*. https://www.verywellmind.com/john-bowlby-biography-1907-1990-2795514.

Crowther, L. (2020, July 30). The Five Stages of Grief and Loss. *Legacy.com*. https://www.legacy.com/advice/the-five-stages-of-grief/.

Dudley, D. (2020, March 29). Seneca. *Encyclopædia Britannica*. https://www.britannica.com/biography/Lucius-Annaeus-Seneca-Roman-philosopher-and-statesman.

Elisabeth Kübler-Ross Biography. *EKR Foundation*. https://www.ekrfoundation.org/elisabeth-kubler-ross/biography/.

Franks, D. (2015, May 26). Understanding: Knowing the Connection Between Anger and Grief. *Crossroads Hospice Charitable Foundation*. https://crhcf.org/insights/understanding-the-anger-caused-by-grief/.

Frazer Consultants. (2020, August 17). Grief Theories Series: Parkes and Bowlby's Four Phases of Grief. *Frazer Consultants*. https://frazerconsultants.com/2018/03/grief-theories-series-parkes-and-bowlbys-four-phases-of-grief/.

Gill, N. (2019, October 25). Does the Serenity Prayer Echo the Greco-Roman Notion of Stoicism? *ThoughtCo*. https://www.thoughtco.com/stoics-and-moral-philosophy-4068536.

Hairston, S. (2019, July 11). How Grief Shows Up In Your Body. *WebMD*. https://www.webmd.com/special-reports/grief-stages/20190711/how-grief-affects-your-body-and-mind.

Holland, K. (2019, January 29). How to Control Anger: 25 Tips to Manage Your Anger and Feel Calmer. *Healthline*. https://www.healthline.com/health/mental-health/how-to-control-anger.

How to Deal With Depression: Wim Hof Method. How to Deal With Depression | *Wim Hof Method.* https://www.wimhofmethod.com/how-to-deal-with-depression.

Jewell, T. (2017, December 8). Depression vs. Complicated Grief. *Healthline.* https://www.healthline.com/health/depression/complicated-grief.

Kashdan, T., & Biswas-Diener, R. (2014, October 20). The Right Way to Get Angry. *Greater Good.* https://greatergood.berkeley.edu/article/item/the_right_way_to_get_angry.

Mayo Clinic. (2016, October 19). What is grief? https://www.mayoclinic.org/patient-visitor-guide/support-groups/what-is-grief.

Nesbitt, A. (2020, October 24). Khabib Nurmagomedov collapsed in tears after beating Justin Gaethje at UFC 254. *USA Today.* https://ftw.usatoday.com/2020/10/ufc-254-khabib-nurmagomedov-cries-after-beating-justin-gaethje.

Perper, R. (2019, July 2). Are You Avoiding Your Grief? *Therapy Changes.* https://therapychanges.com/blog/2018/03/avoiding-grief/.

Popova, M. (2018, November 13). Epictetus on Love and Loss: The Stoic Strategy for Surviving Heartbreak. *Brain Pickings.* https://www.brainpickings.org/2018/08/26/epictetus-love-loss/.

Popova, M. (2018, November 13). Marcus Aurelius on Mortality and the Key to Living Fully. *Brain Pickings.* https://www.brainpickings.org/2015/11/18/marcus-aurelius-meditations-mortality/.

Popova, M. (2018, November 13). Seneca on Grief and the Key to Resilience in the Face of Loss: An Extraordinary Letter to His Mother. *Brain Pickings*. https://www.brainpickings.org/2017/05/02/seneca-consolation-to-helvia/.

Pritchard, E. (2018, July 17). 20 physical, behavioural and emotional symptoms of bereavement and how to overcome them. *Country Living*. https://www.countryliving.com/uk/wellbeing/a21549981/physical-emotional-behavioural-symptoms-grief-bereavement-how-overcome/.

Romm, C. (2014, September 11). Understanding How Grief Weakens the Body. *The Atlantic*. https://www.theatlantic.com/health/archive/2014/09/understanding-how-grief-weakens-the-body/380006/.

Ropchan, J. (2013, March 14). 5 Common Grief Avoidance Patterns - *Your Tribute*. http://resources.yourtribute.com/grief-and-loss/grief-avoidance-patterns/.

Schwartz, A. The Difference Between Grief and Depression, The DSM V. *Mental Help*. https://www.mentalhelp.net/blogs/the-difference-between-grief-and-depression-the-dsm-v/.

The Science Behind The Wim Hof Method | *Wim Hof Method*. https://www.wimhofmethod.com/science.

Shermer, M. (2008, November 1). Five Fallacies of Grief: Debunking Psychological Stages. *Scientific American*. https://www.scientificamerican.com/article/five-fallacies-of-grief/.

Sinicki, A. (2018, November 5). Explaining the Wim Hof Method. *The Bioneer*. https://www.thebioneer.com/explaining-wim-hof-method/.

A Stoic Response to Grief. *Daily Stoic*. (2017, September 25). https://dailystoic.com/stoic-response-grief/.

Stoicism And Depression Teach A Valuable Lesson About Lockdown Grief. *MindThatEgo*. (2020, June 2). https://www.mindthatego.com/negative-visualisation/.

UHC Newsroom. (2020, June 17). Anxiety-Fighting Foods that May Help Bring Calm, Balance. *Newsroom*. https://newsroom.uhc.com/health/anti-anxiety.html?Source=Google.

What Is Stoicism? A Definition & 9 Stoic Exercises To Get You Started. *Daily Stoic*. (2020, May 8). https://dailystoic.com/what-is-stoicism-a-definition-3-stoic-exercises-to-get-you-started/.

Who Is Epictetus? From Slave To World's Most Sought After Philosopher. *Daily Stoic*. (2020, August 31). https://dailystoic.com/epictetus/.

Who Is Marcus Aurelius? Getting To Know The Roman Emperor. *Daily Stoic*. (2020, August 31). https://dailystoic.com/marcus-aurelius/.

Who Is Seneca? Inside The Mind of The World's Most Interesting Stoic. *Daily Stoic*. (2020, August 19). https://dailystoic.com/seneca/.

Wikimedia Foundation. (2020, October 21). Five stages of grief. *Wikipedia*. https://en.wikipedia.org/wiki/Five_stages_of_grief.

Wolfelt, A. (2018, October 17). Grieving vs. Mourning: *TAPS. taps tragedy assistance program survivors.* https://www.taps.org/articles/24-3/grieving-vs-mourning.